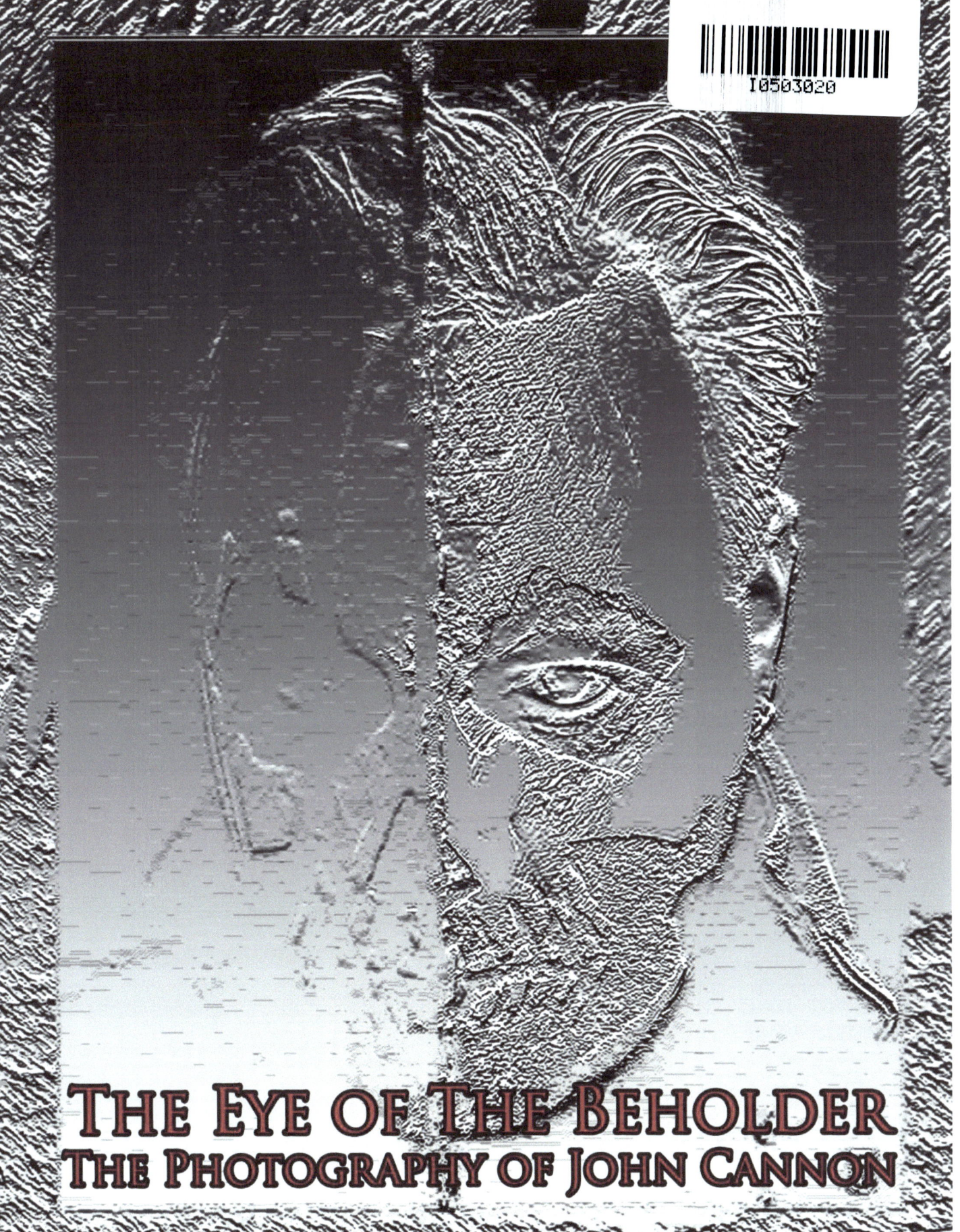

THE EYE OF THE BEHOLDER
THE PHOTOGRAPHY OF JOHN CANNON

For information about custom editions, special sales, signings, premium, and corporate purchases please contact Sound Impressions (973) 263-0521

Publisher: Sound Impressions
            Attn: Publishing
            PO Box 754
            Boonton, NJ 07005

            http://www.soundimp.net

Layout: Jason R. Koba

Photographes by: John Cannon

This is dedicated to my friends and family...

to those who have stuck beside me through the worst of the worst and the best of the best.

I also dedicate this to my enemies, for you have been a small part of my vision and

gave me strength to carry on and prove you wrong...fyi I still hate you.

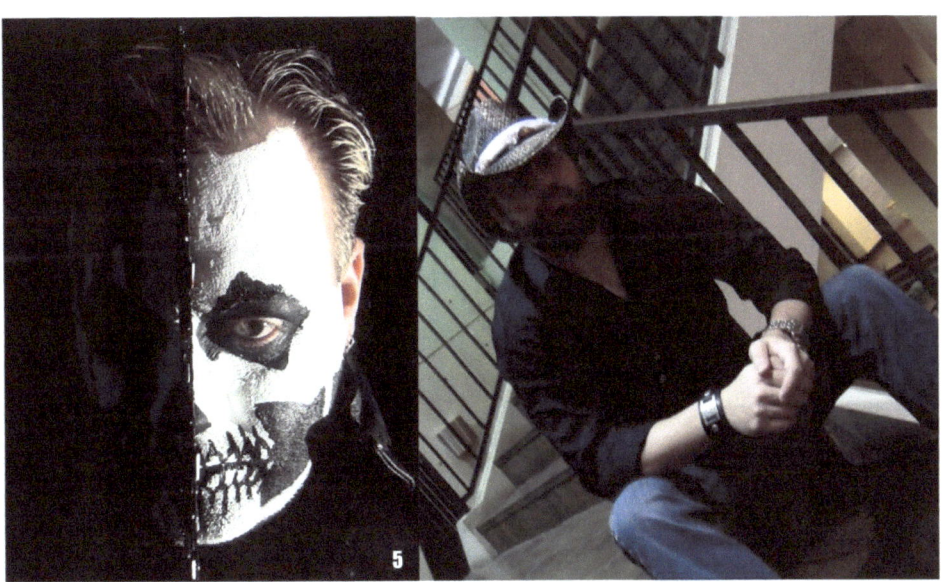

Beauty is in the eye of the beholder…no truer words have ever been written or spoken. The way an individual looks at life through their eyes changes as they travel this road called life. From the innocence we view as a child to the experience we view as an elder, the things we see along the way make up what we know and believe. To some a field of flowers is the most beautiful sight in the world while others may see the beauty in a graveyard…the interpretation of the view is in the beholder. In this book you will see of my interpretations and my views I have seen in life and have been lucky enough to capture in photo. I hope you enjoy it and that it inspires you to let your vision and interpretation be shared by all.

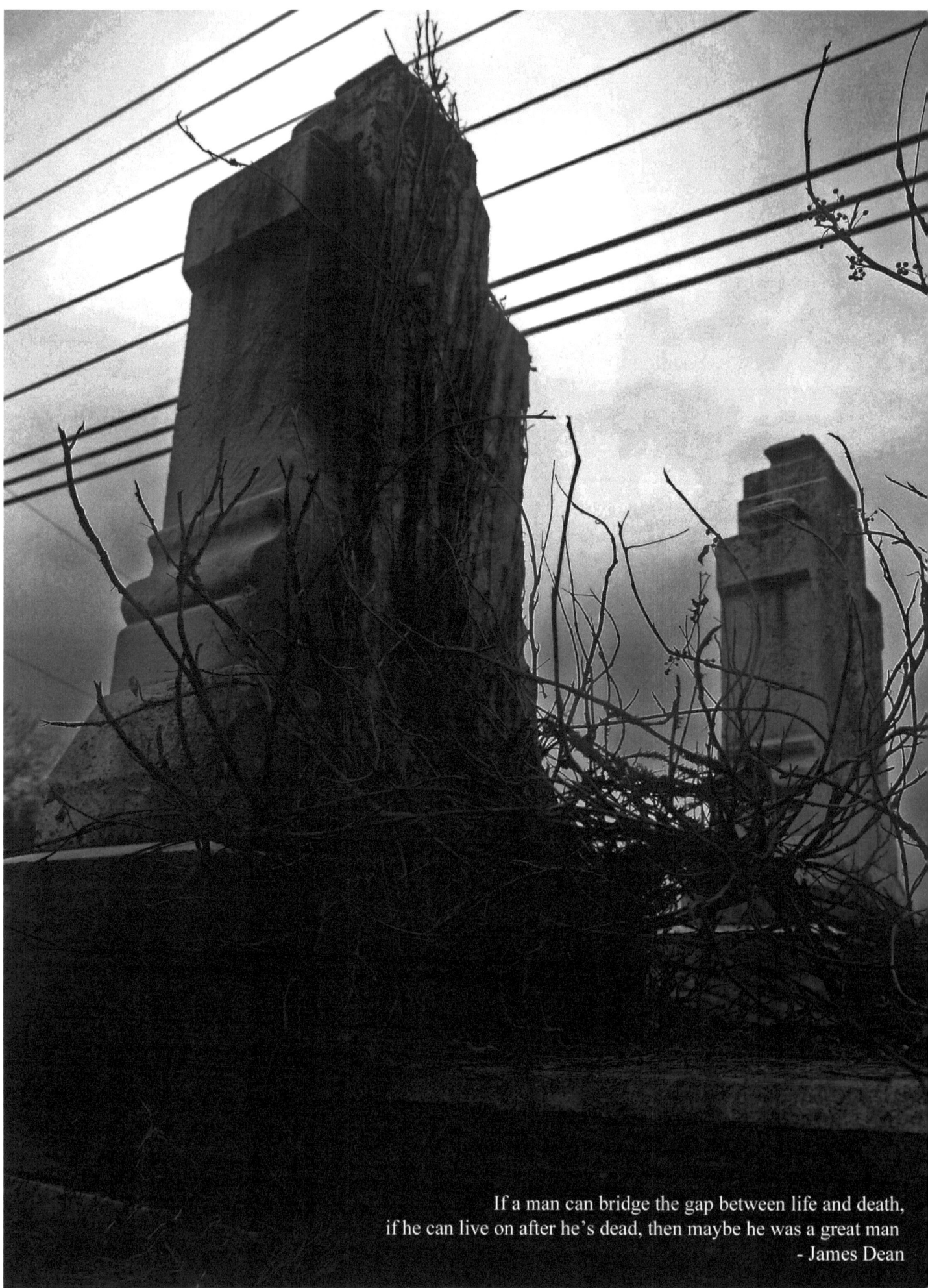

If a man can bridge the gap between life and death,
if he can live on after he's dead, then maybe he was a great man
- James Dean

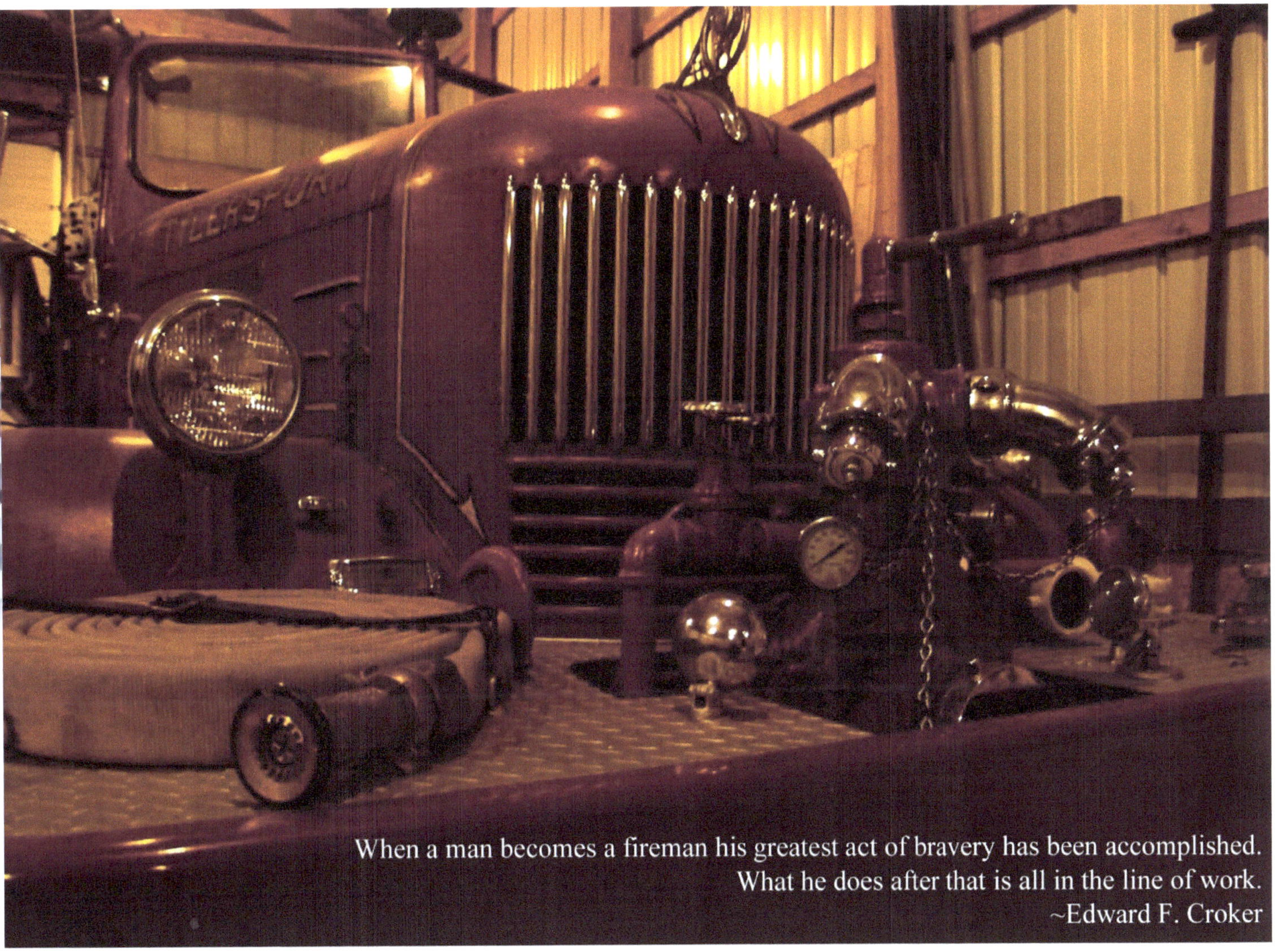

When a man becomes a fireman his greatest act of bravery has been accomplished.
What he does after that is all in the line of work.
~Edward F. Croker

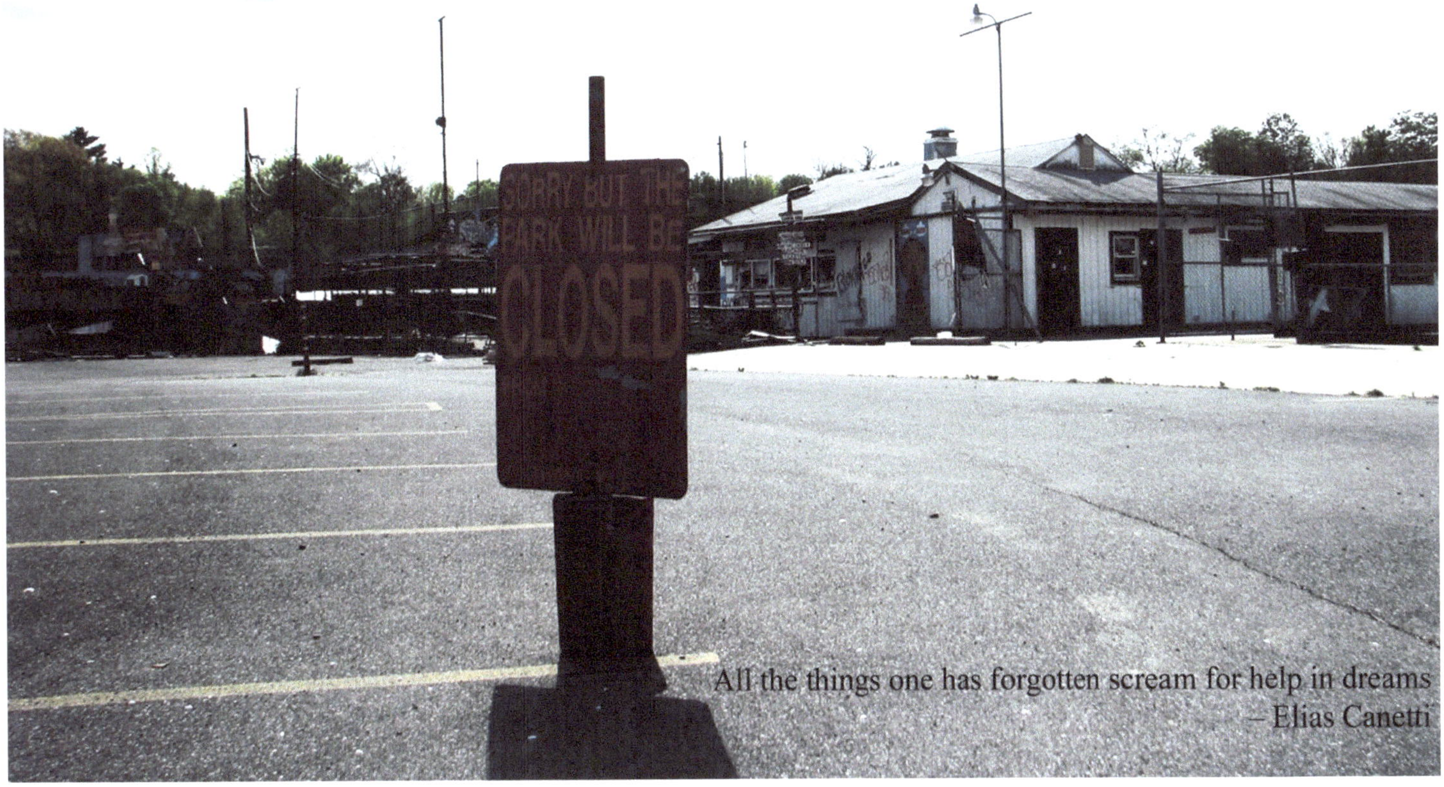

All the things one has forgotten scream for help in dreams
– Elias Canetti

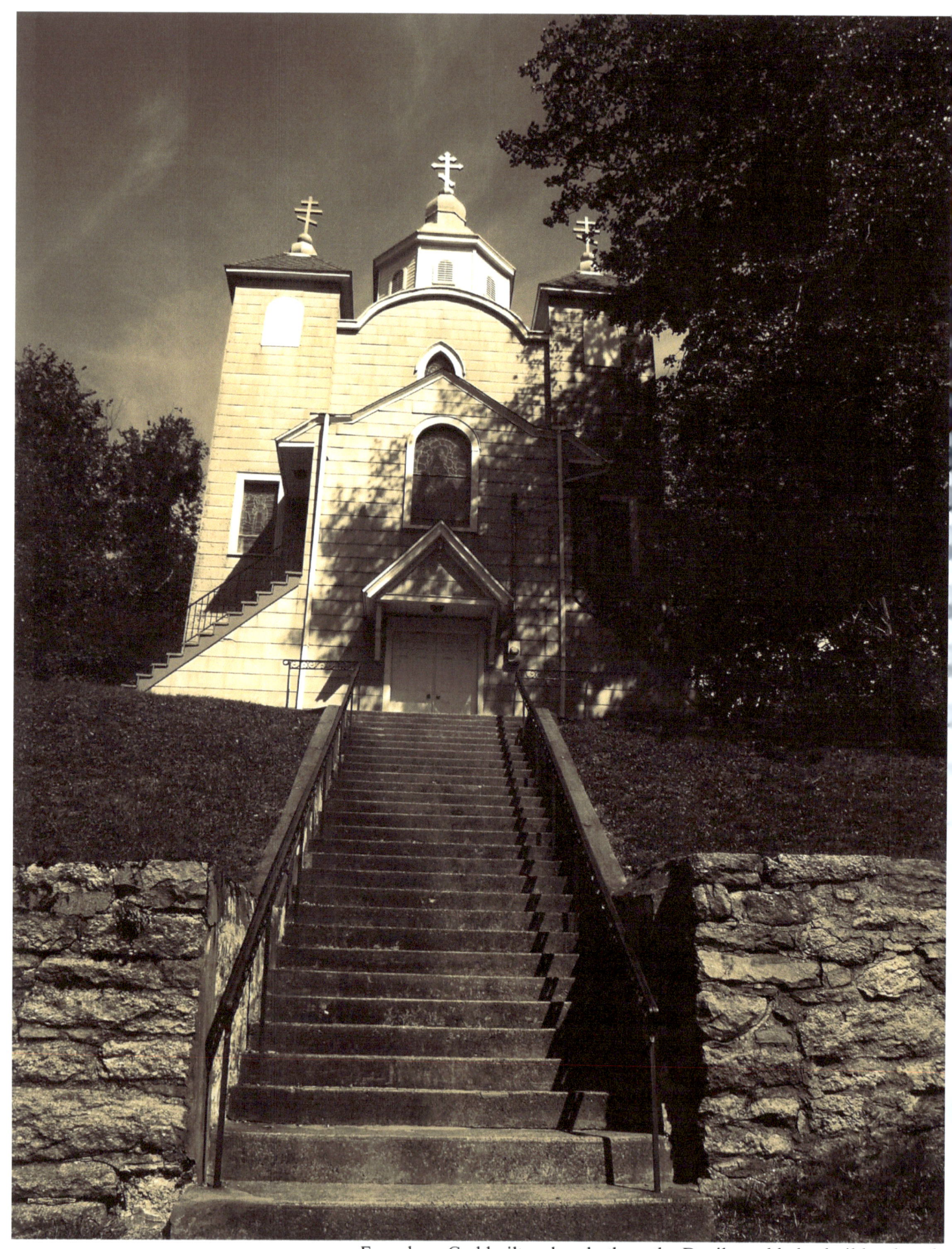

For where God built a church, there the Devil would also build a chapel
– Martin Luther

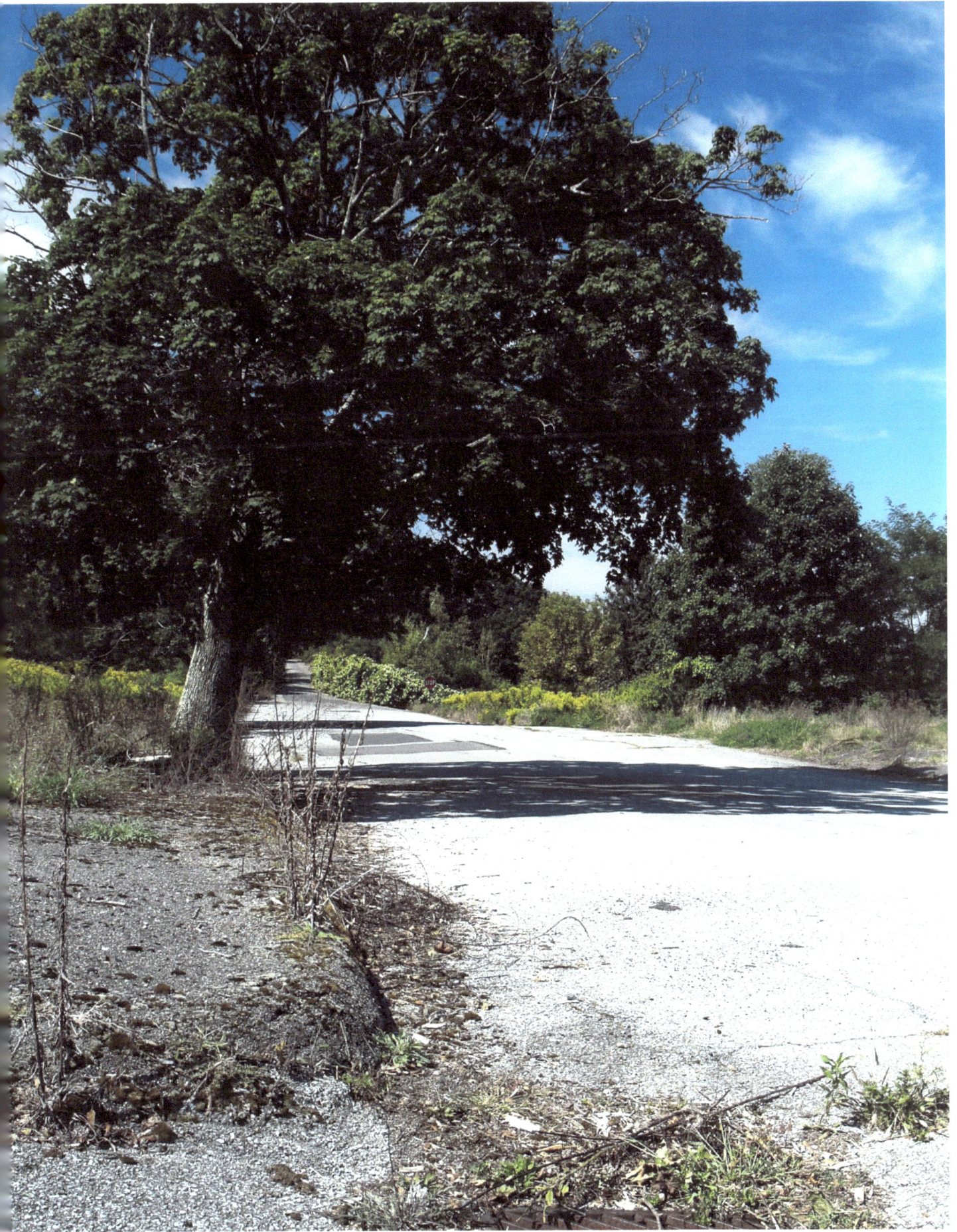

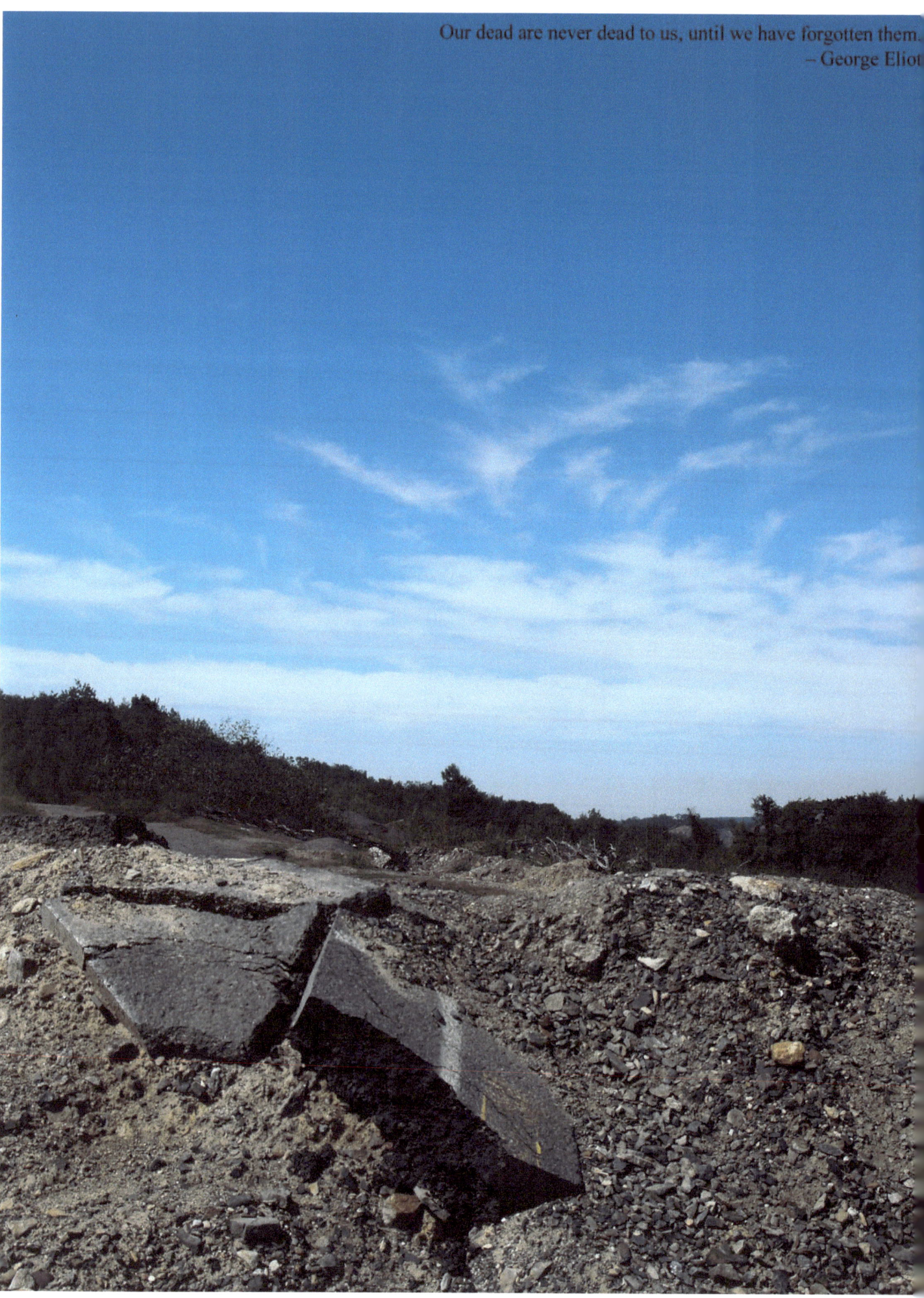

Our dead are never dead to us, until we have forgotten them.
– George Eliot

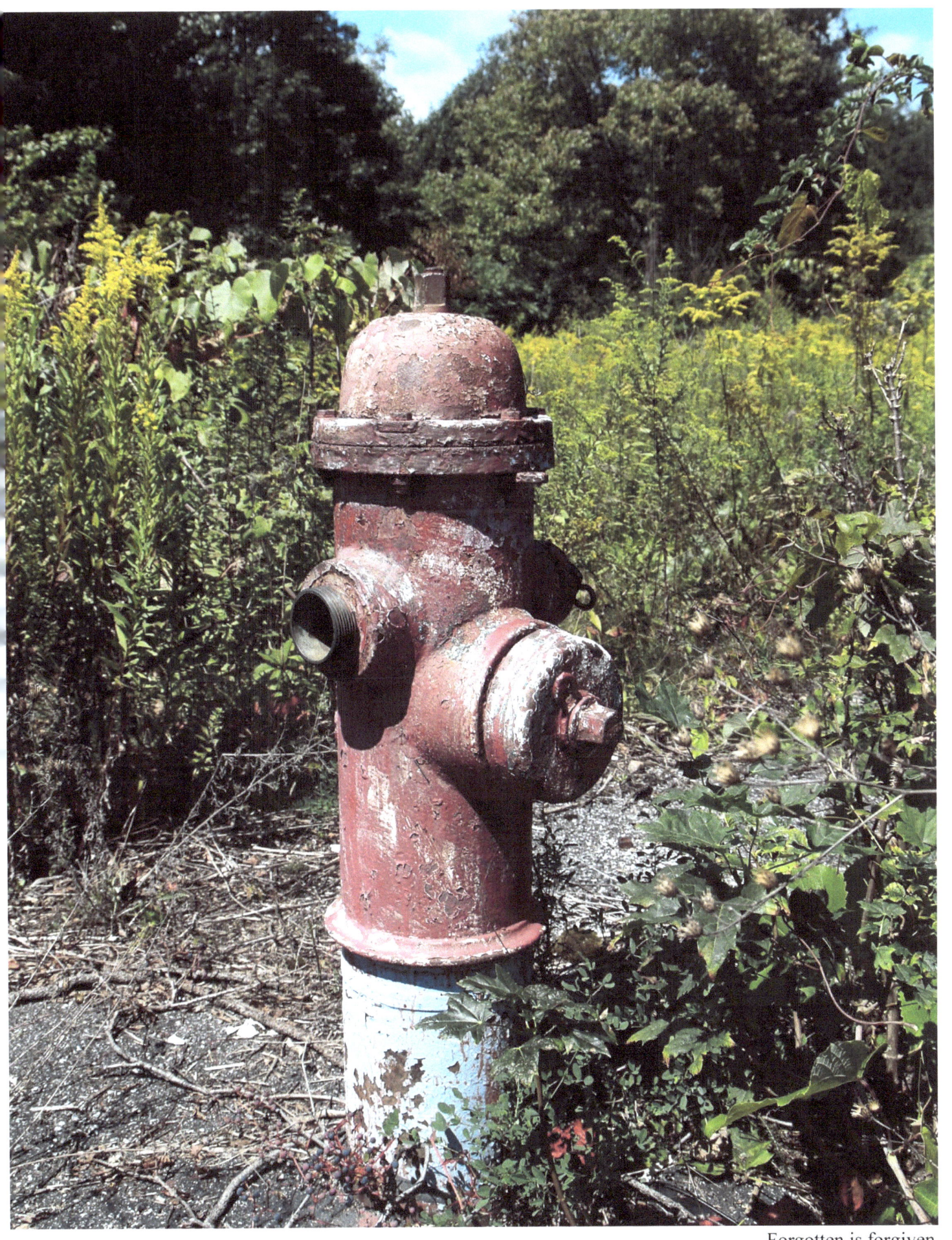

Forgotten is forgiven
– F. Scott Fitzgerald

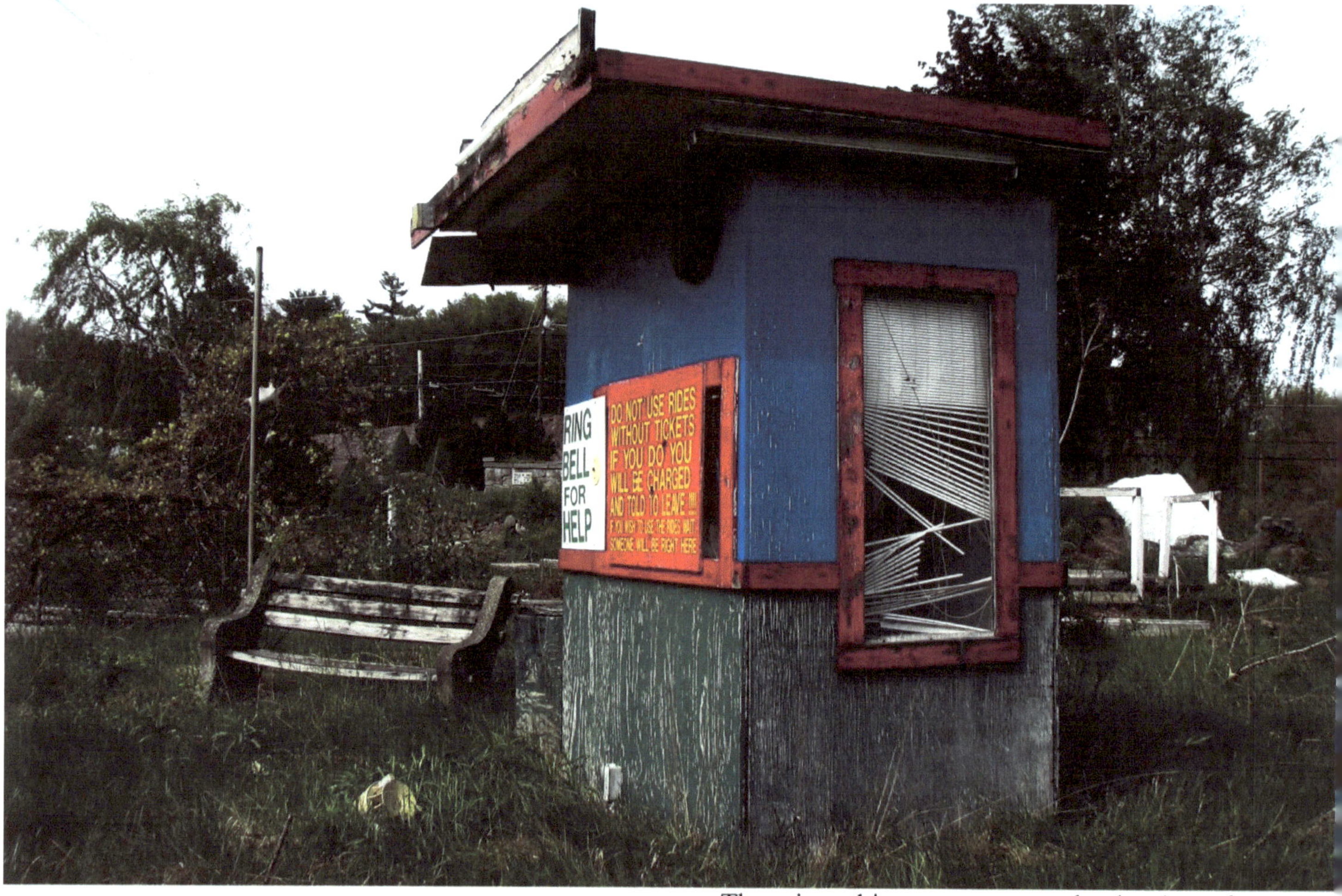

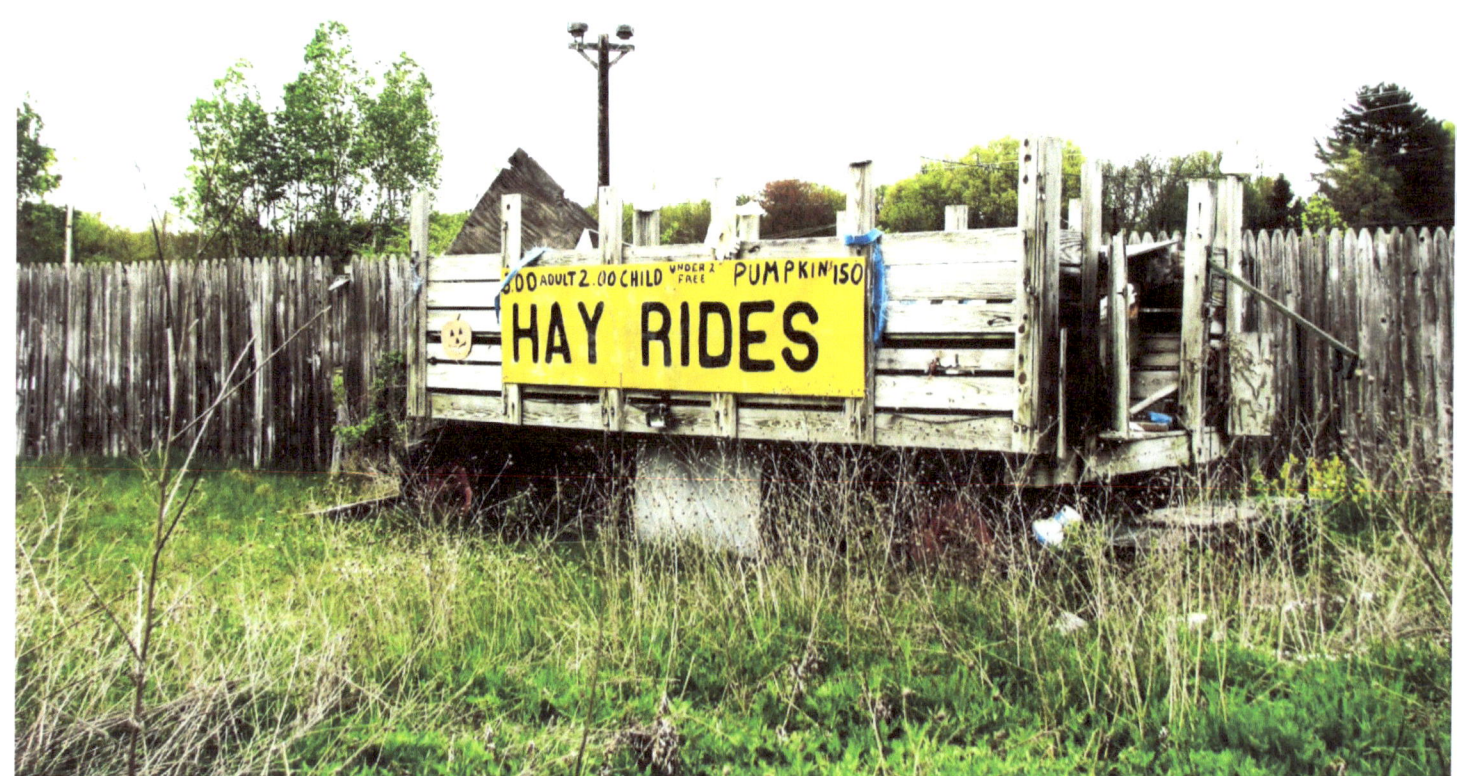

There is nothing new except what has been forgotten
– Marie Antoinette

Education is what survives when what has been learned has been forgotten – B.F. Skinner

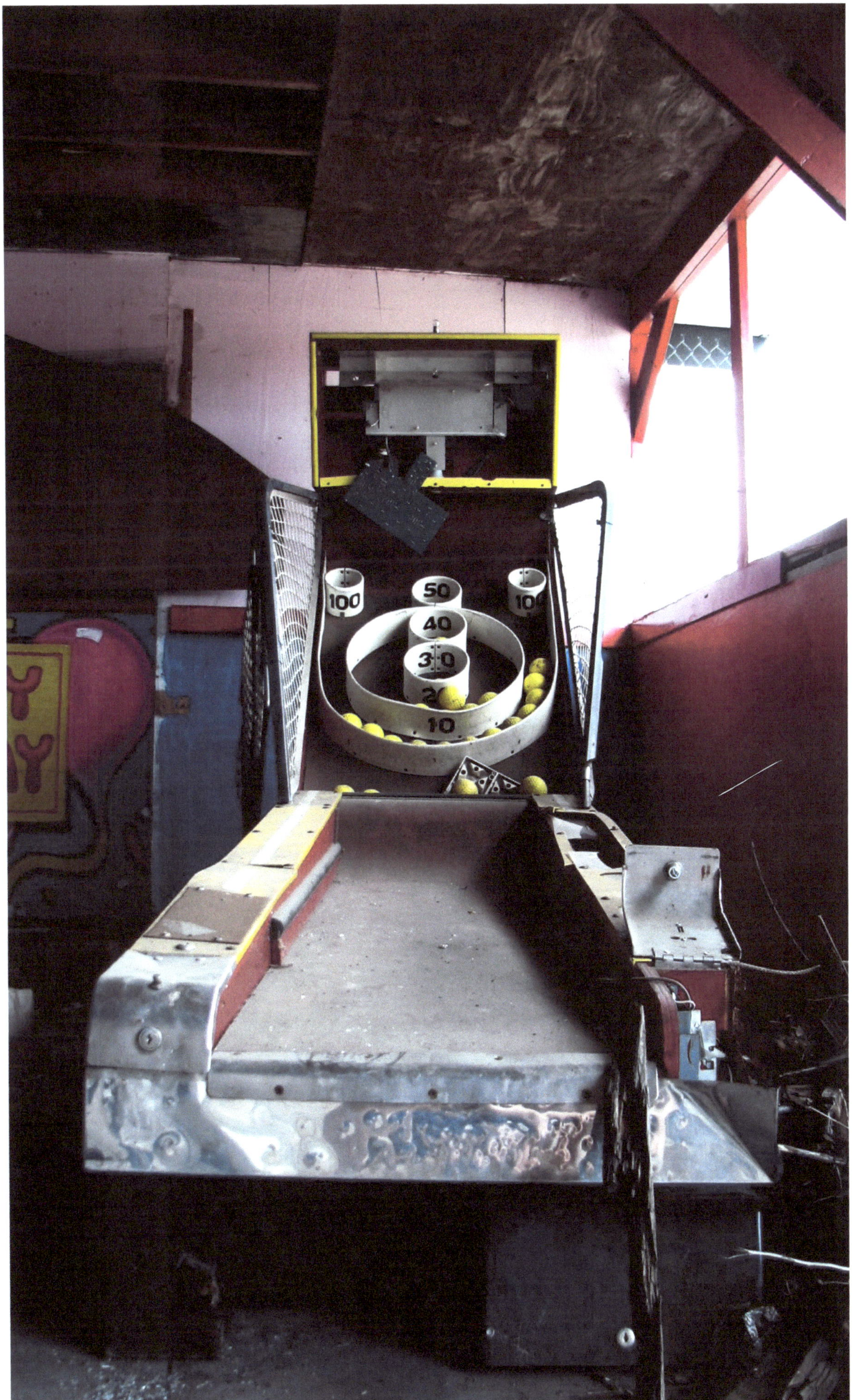

Most reputations are not ruined but forgotten – Mason Cooley

I am an expert of electricity. My father occupied the chair of applied electricity at the state prison.
– W.C. Fields

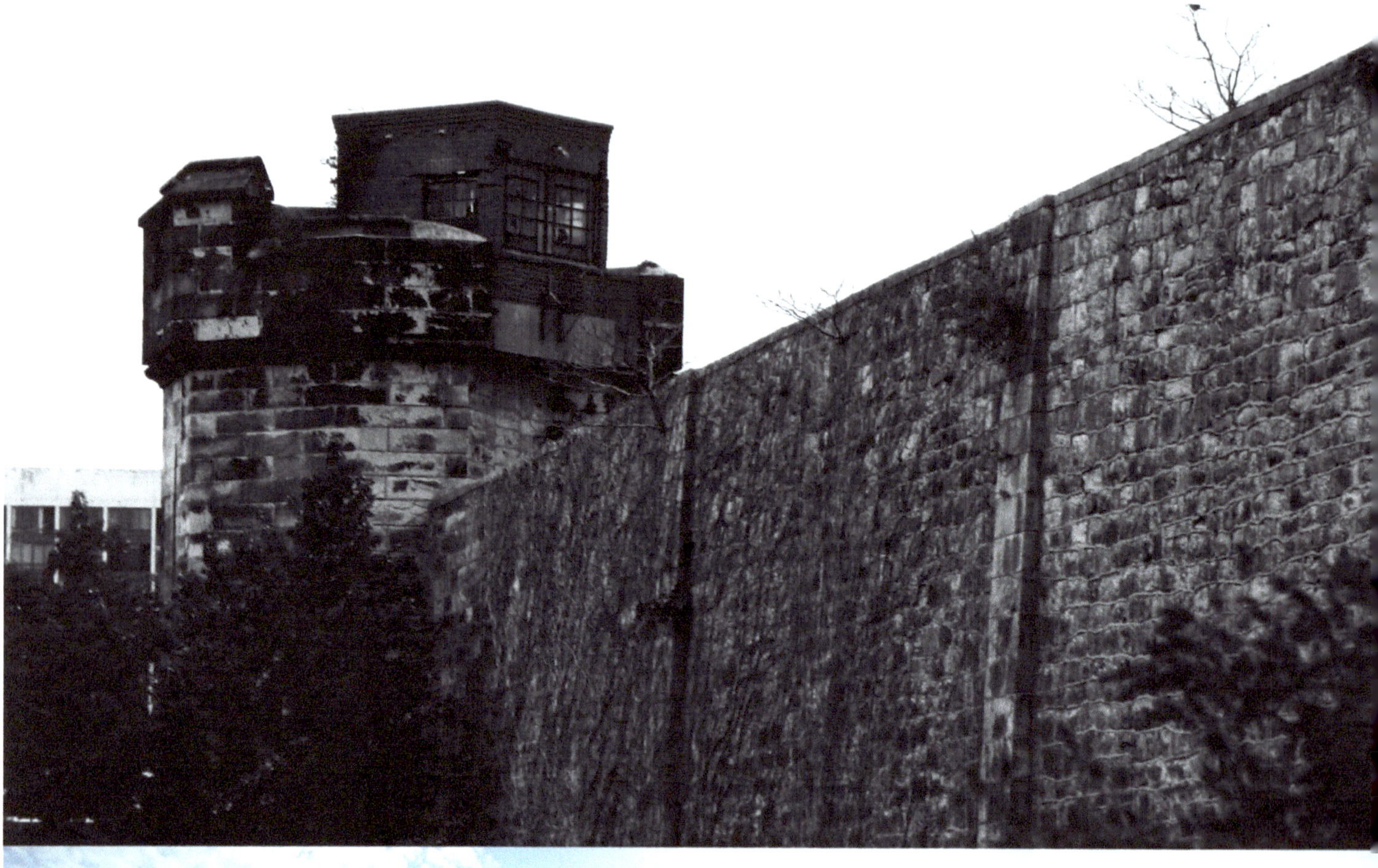

Every gun that is made, every warship launched, every rocket fired, signifies in the final sense a theft from those who hunger and are not fed, those who are cold and are not clothed.
– Dwight D. Eisenhower

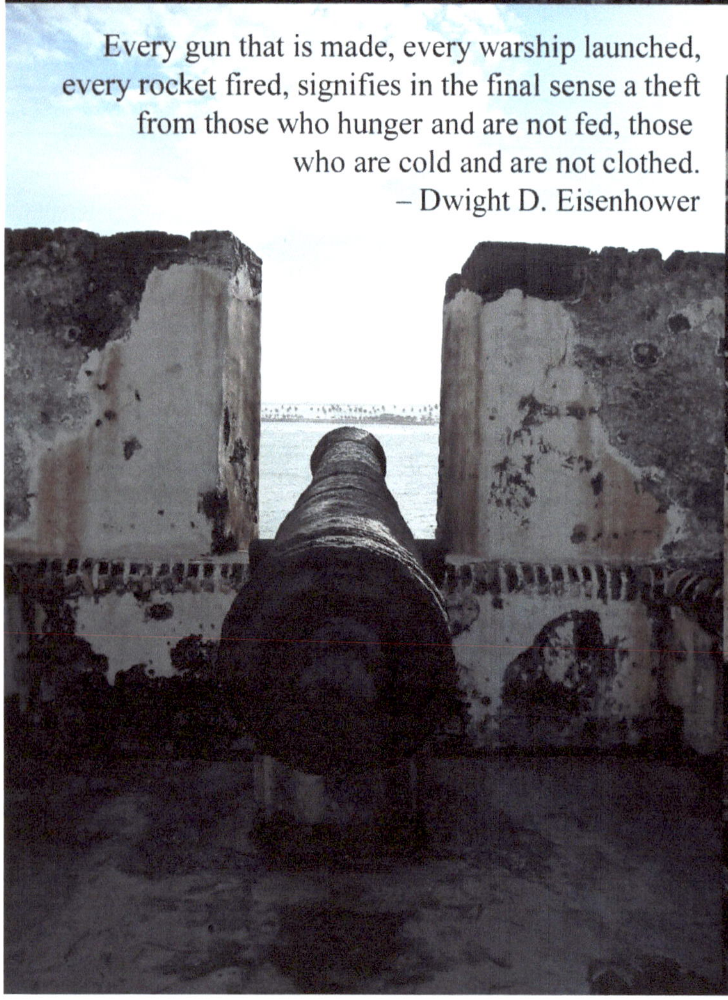

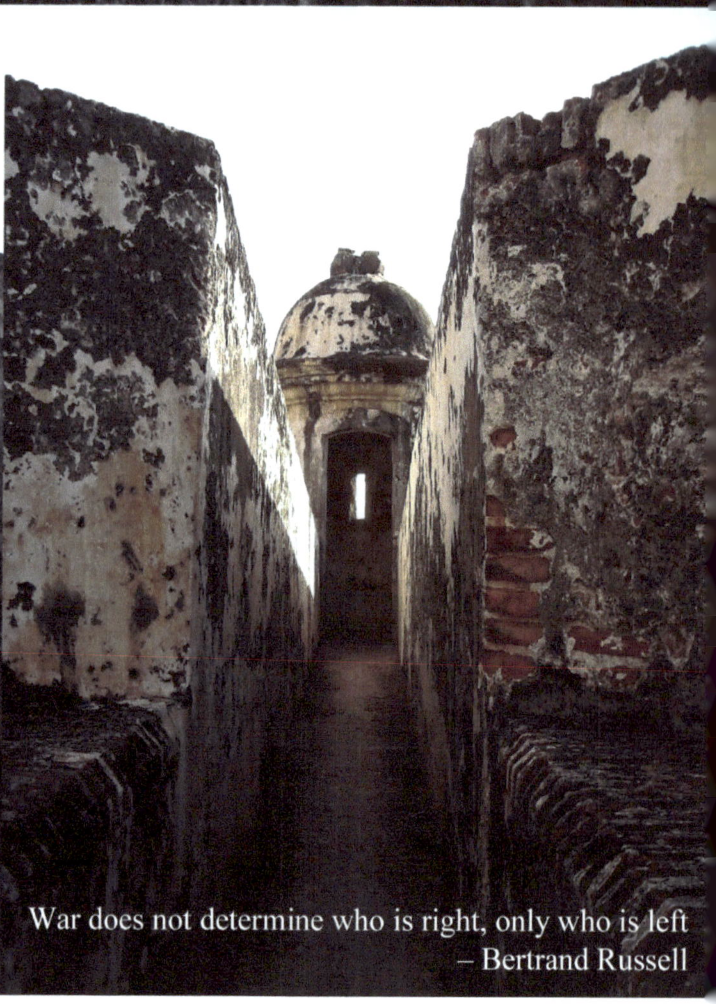

War does not determine who is right, only who is left
– Bertrand Russell

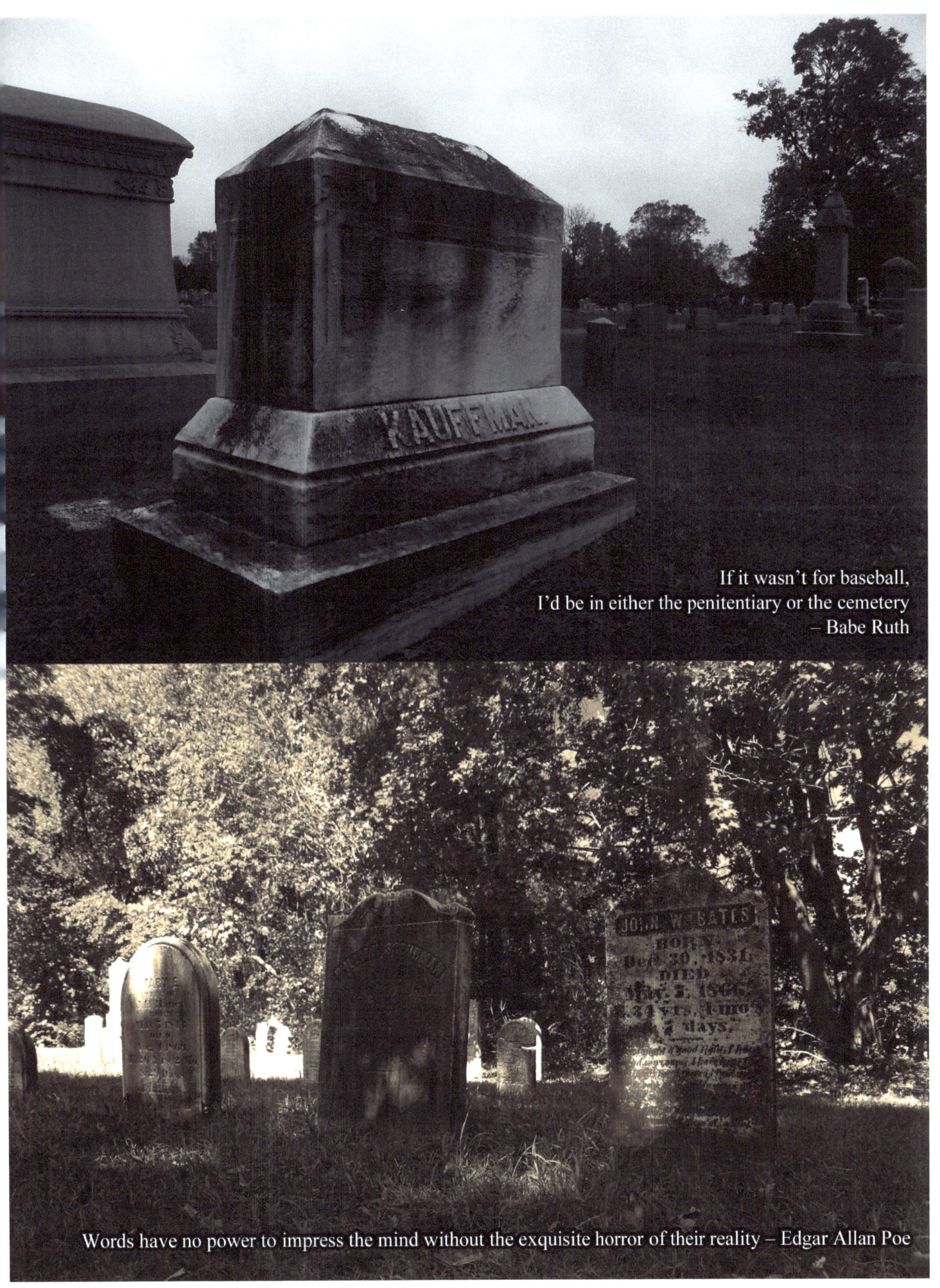

If it wasn't for baseball,
I'd be in either the penitentiary or the cemetery
– Babe Ruth

Words have no power to impress the mind without the exquisite horror of their reality – Edgar Allan Poe

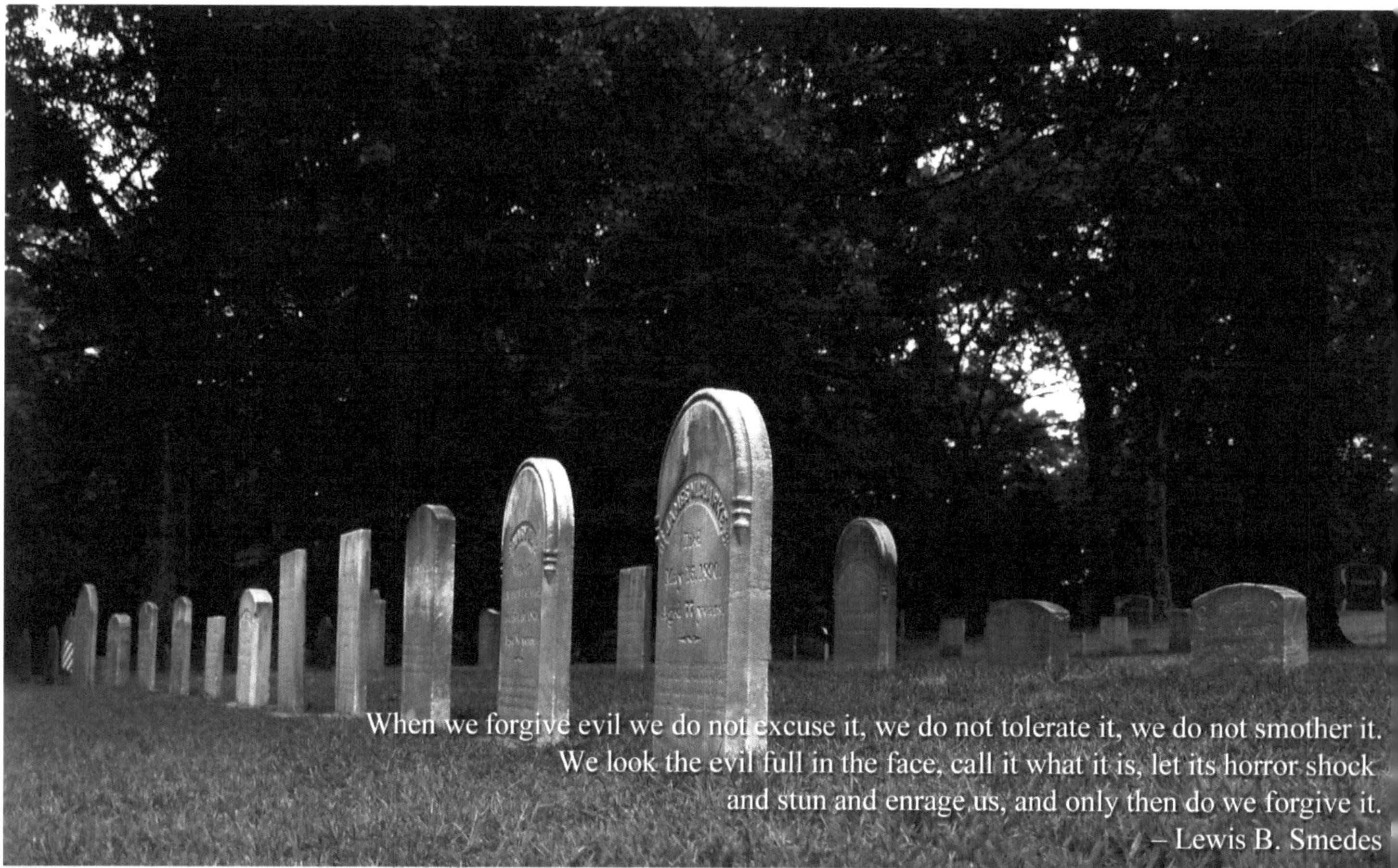

When we forgive evil we do not excuse it, we do not tolerate it, we do not smother it.
We look the evil full in the face, call it what it is, let its horror shock
and stun and enrage us, and only then do we forgive it.
— Lewis B. Smedes

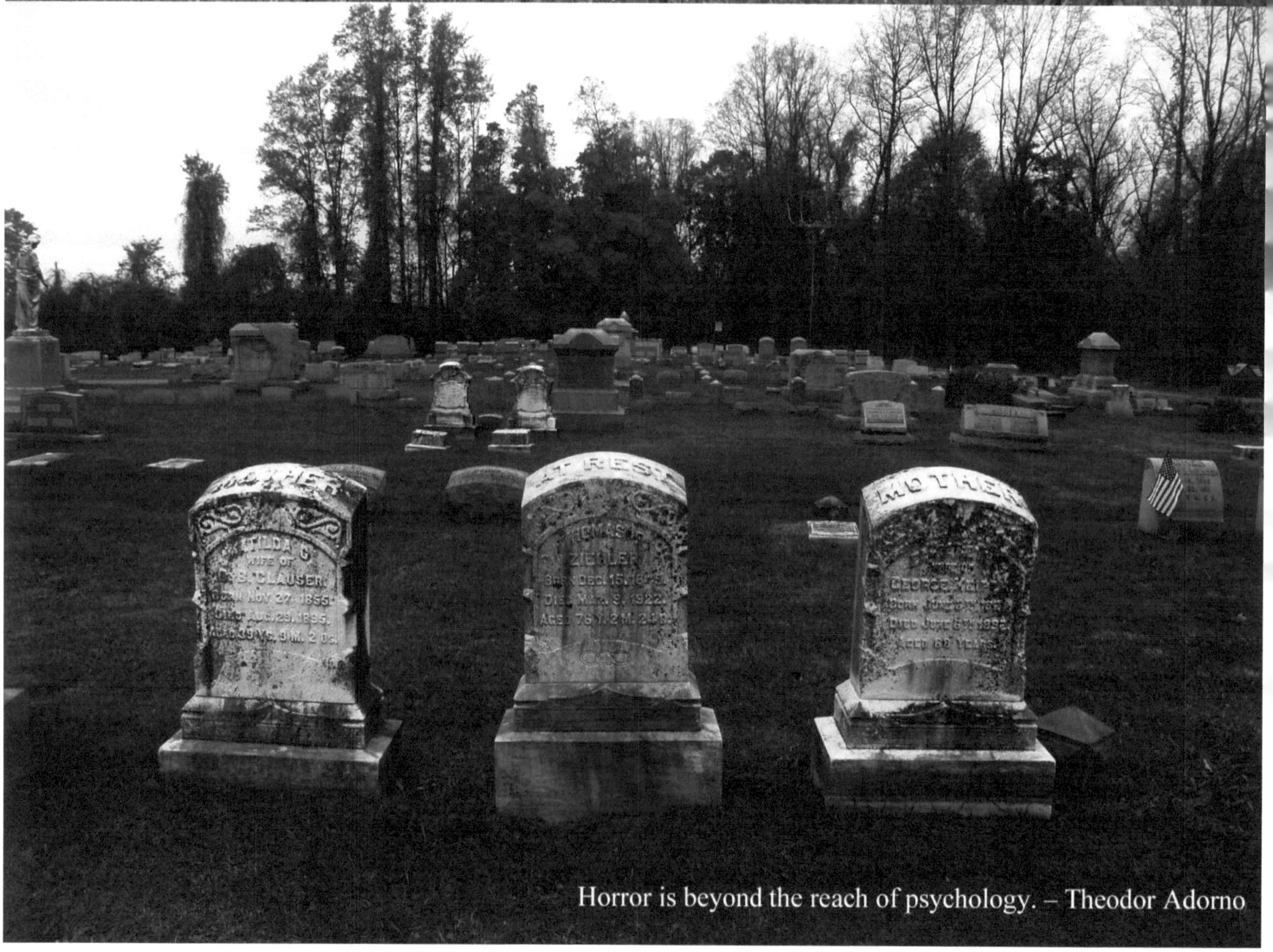

Horror is beyond the reach of psychology. – Theodor Adorno

Horror is the natural reaction to the last 5,000 years of history – Robert Anton Wilson

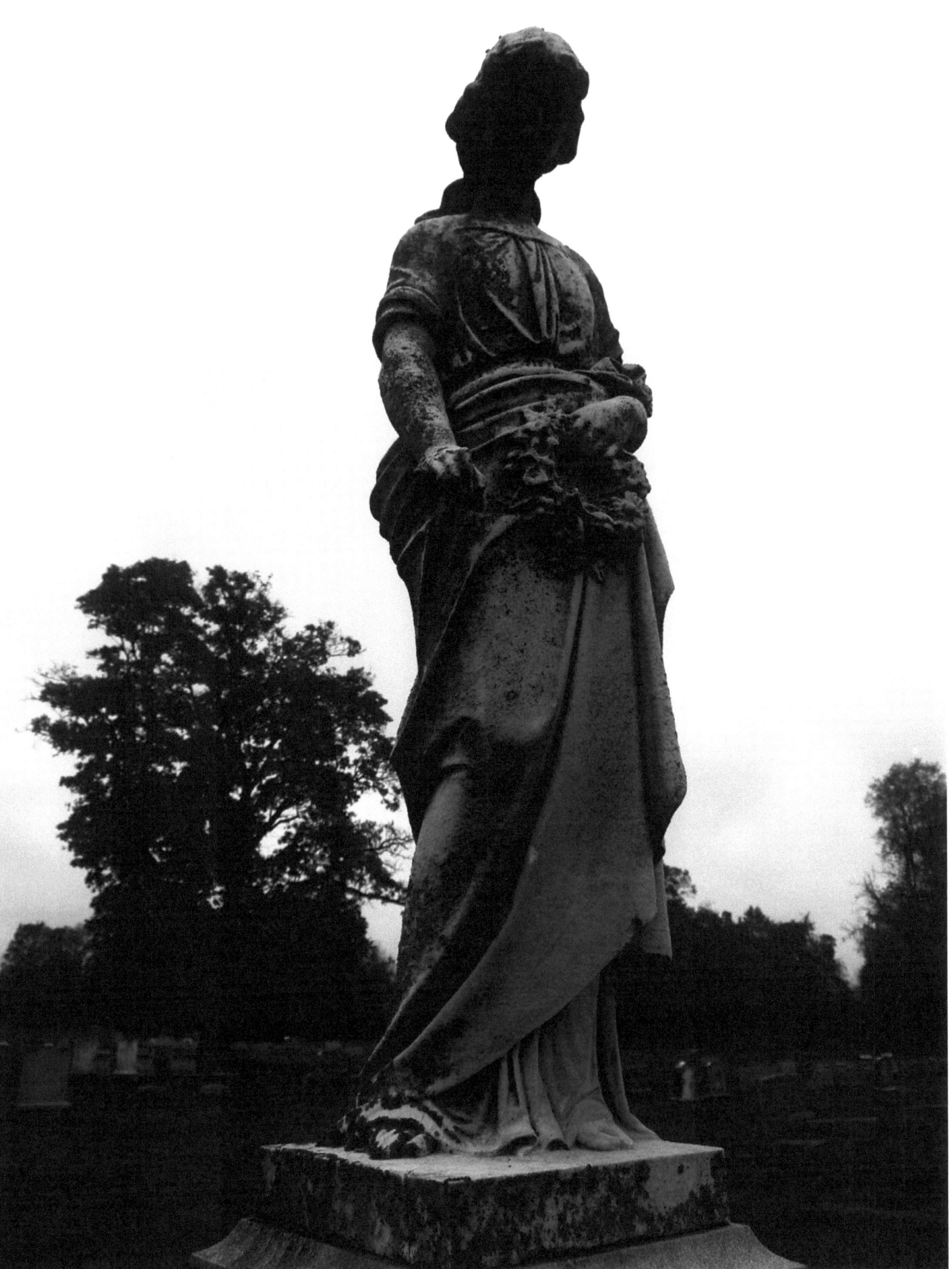

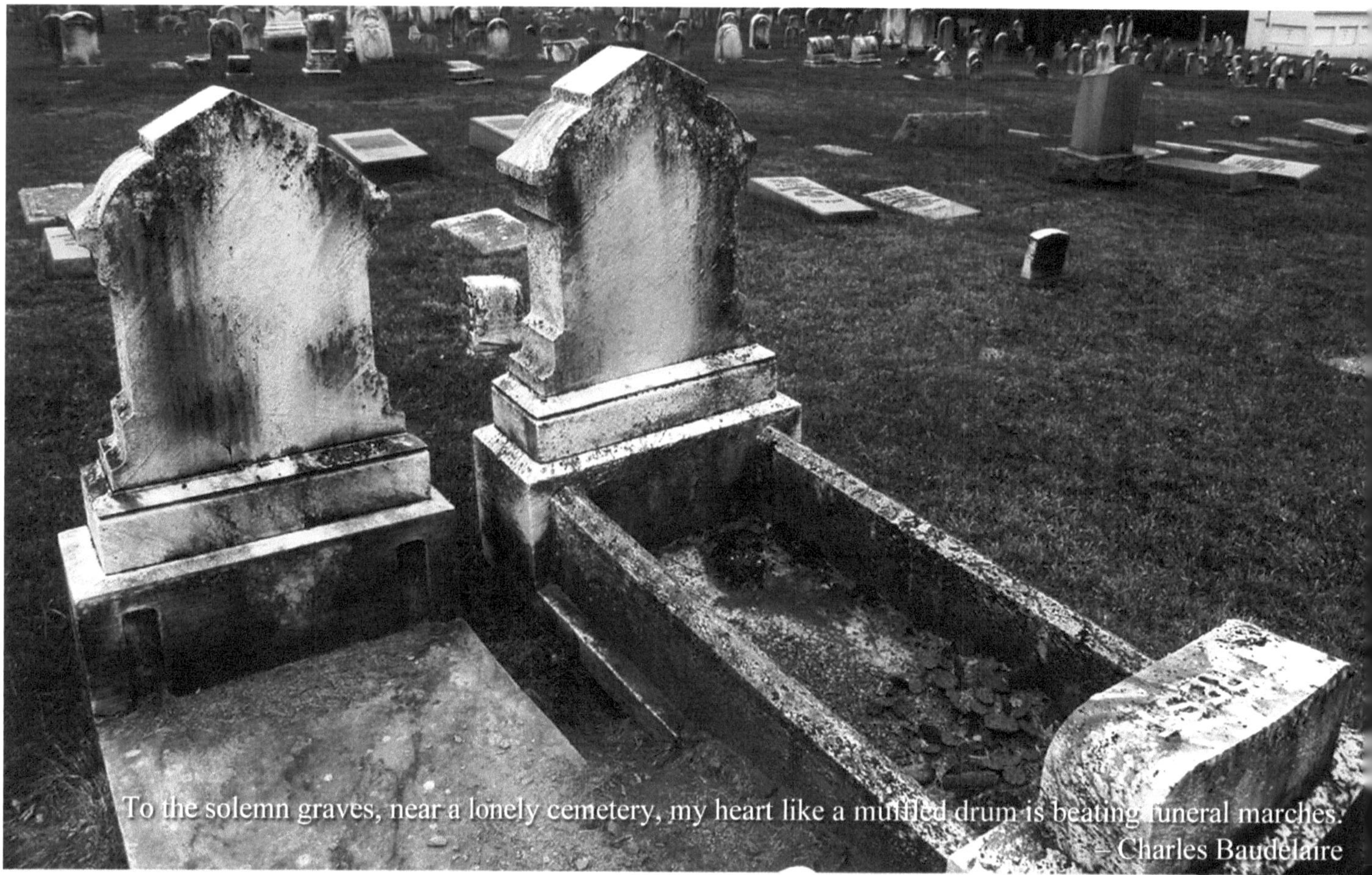

To the solemn graves, near a lonely cemetery, my heart like a muffled drum is beating funeral marches.
— Charles Baudelaire

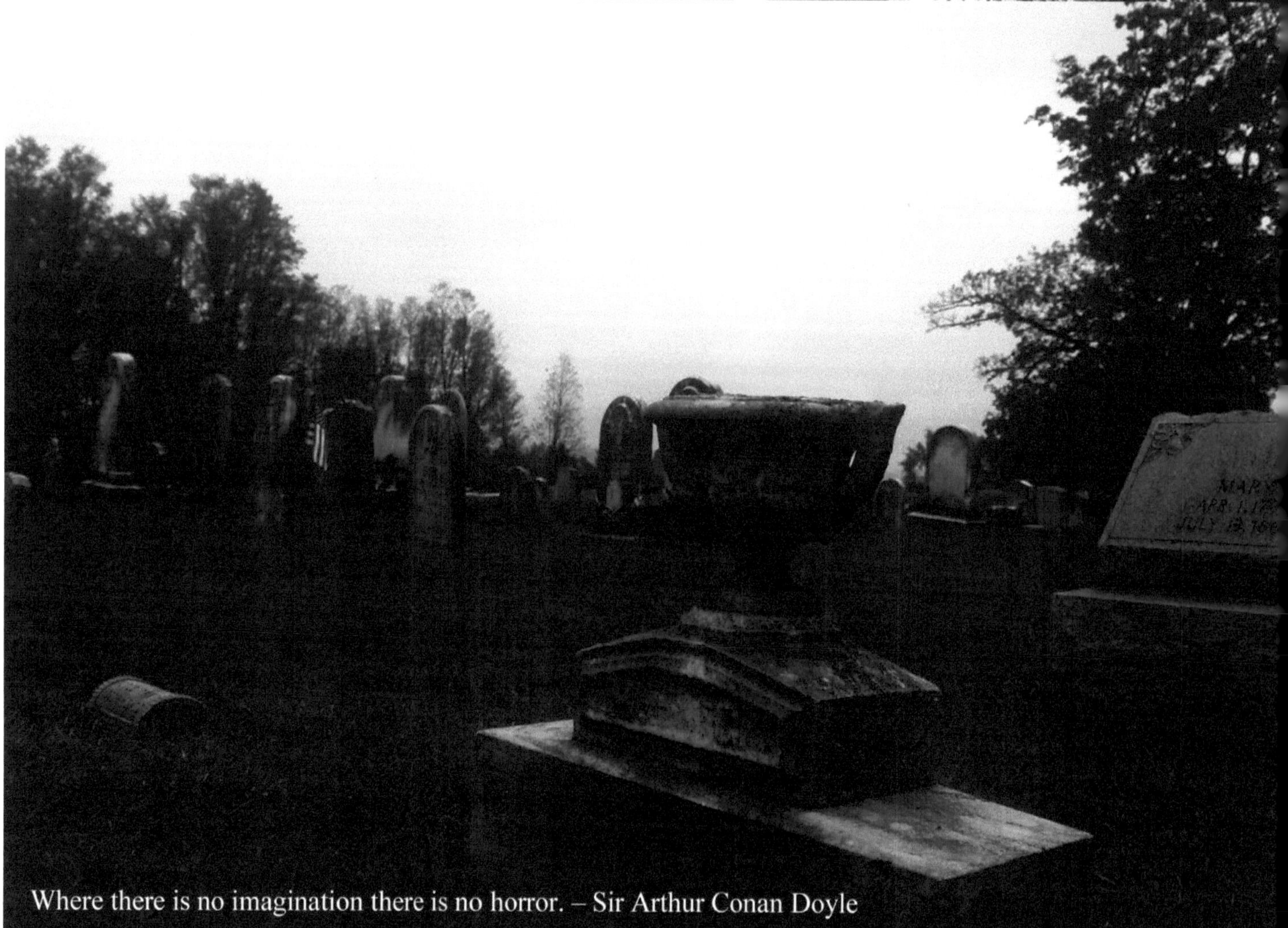

Where there is no imagination there is no horror. — Sir Arthur Conan Doyle

You can't make people believe in you if you play a horror part with your tongue in your cheek.
– Bela Lugosi

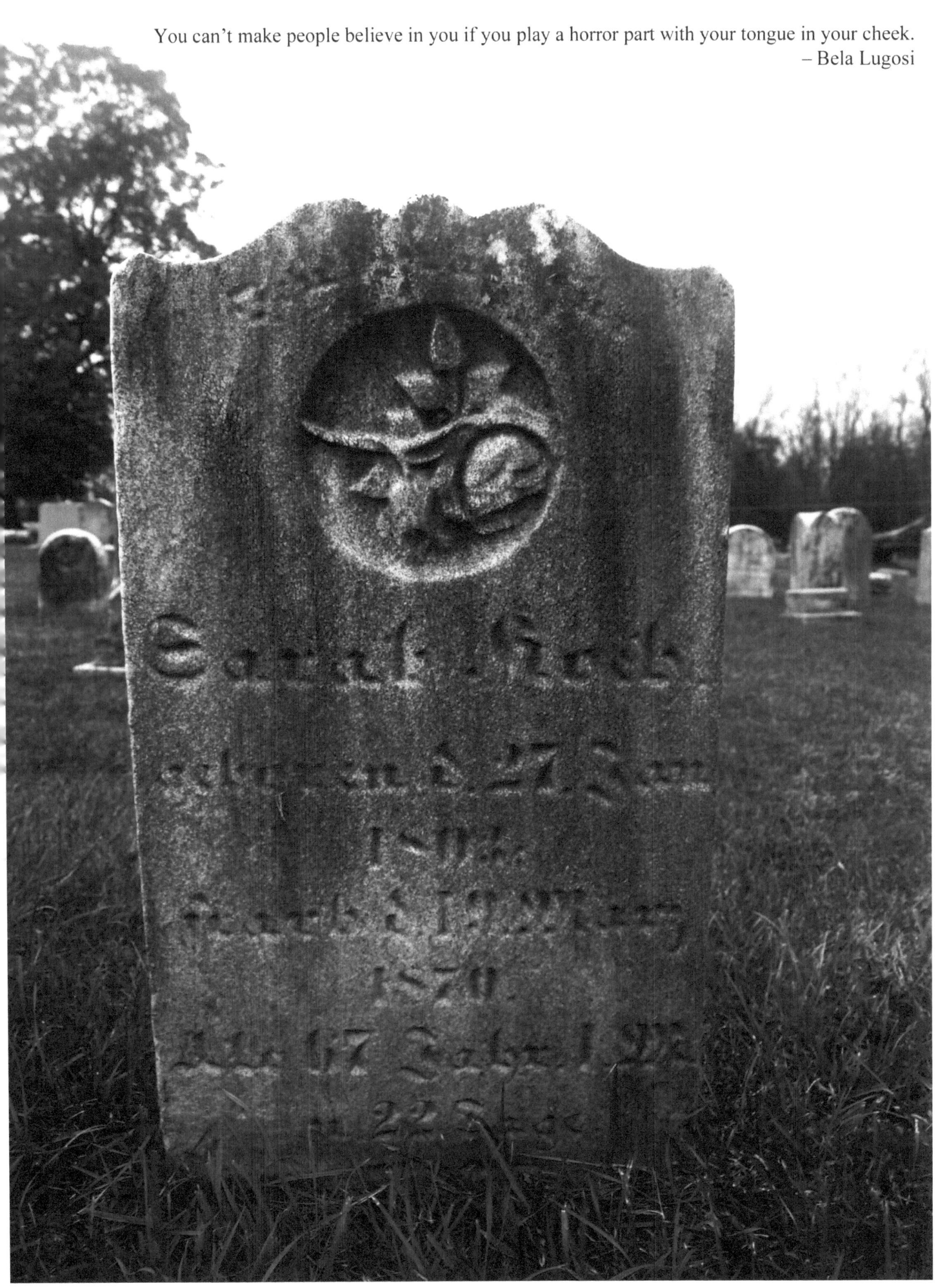

The wing of the Falcon brings him to the king, the wing of the Crow brings him to the cemetery
– Muhammad Iqbal

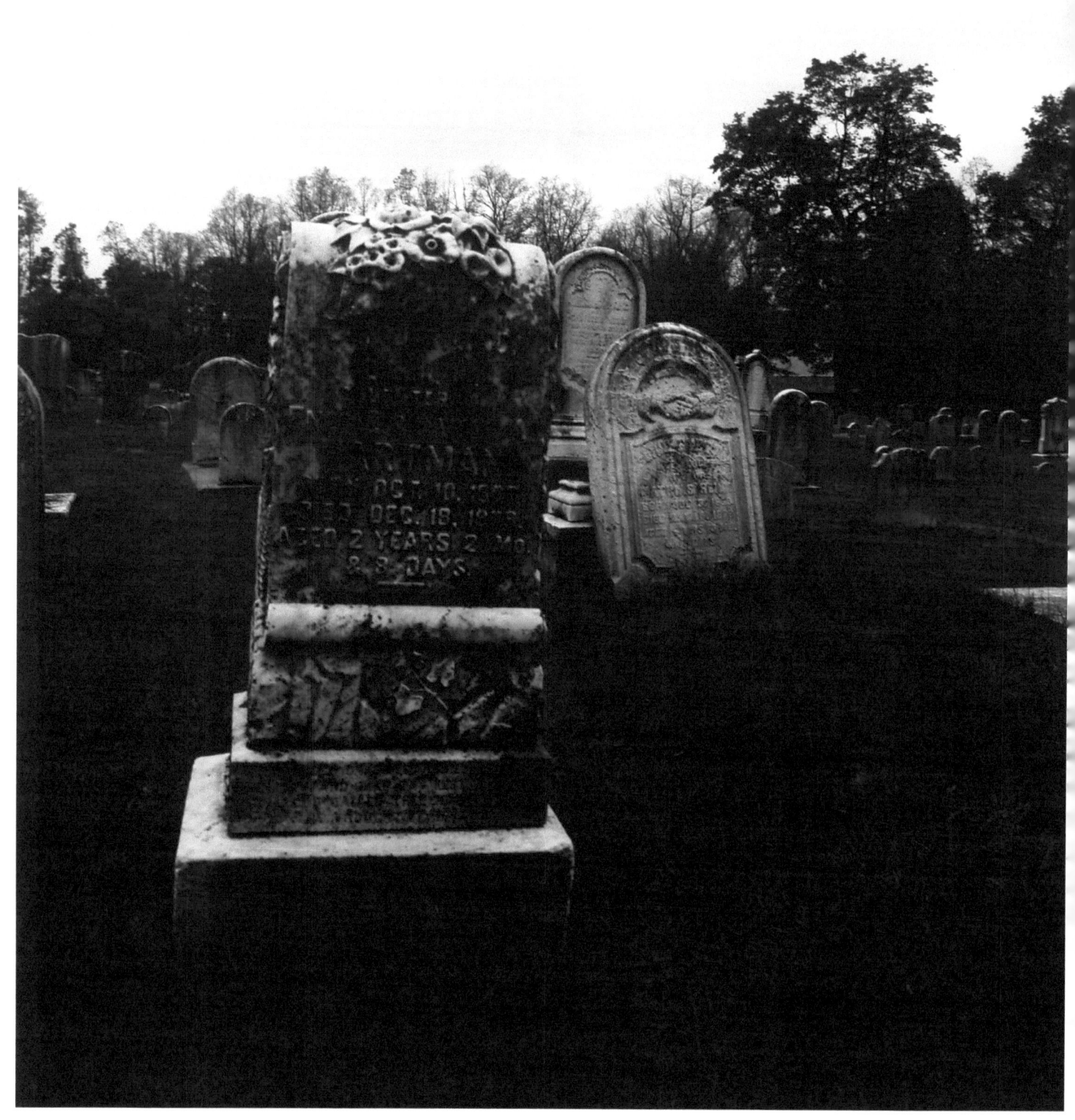

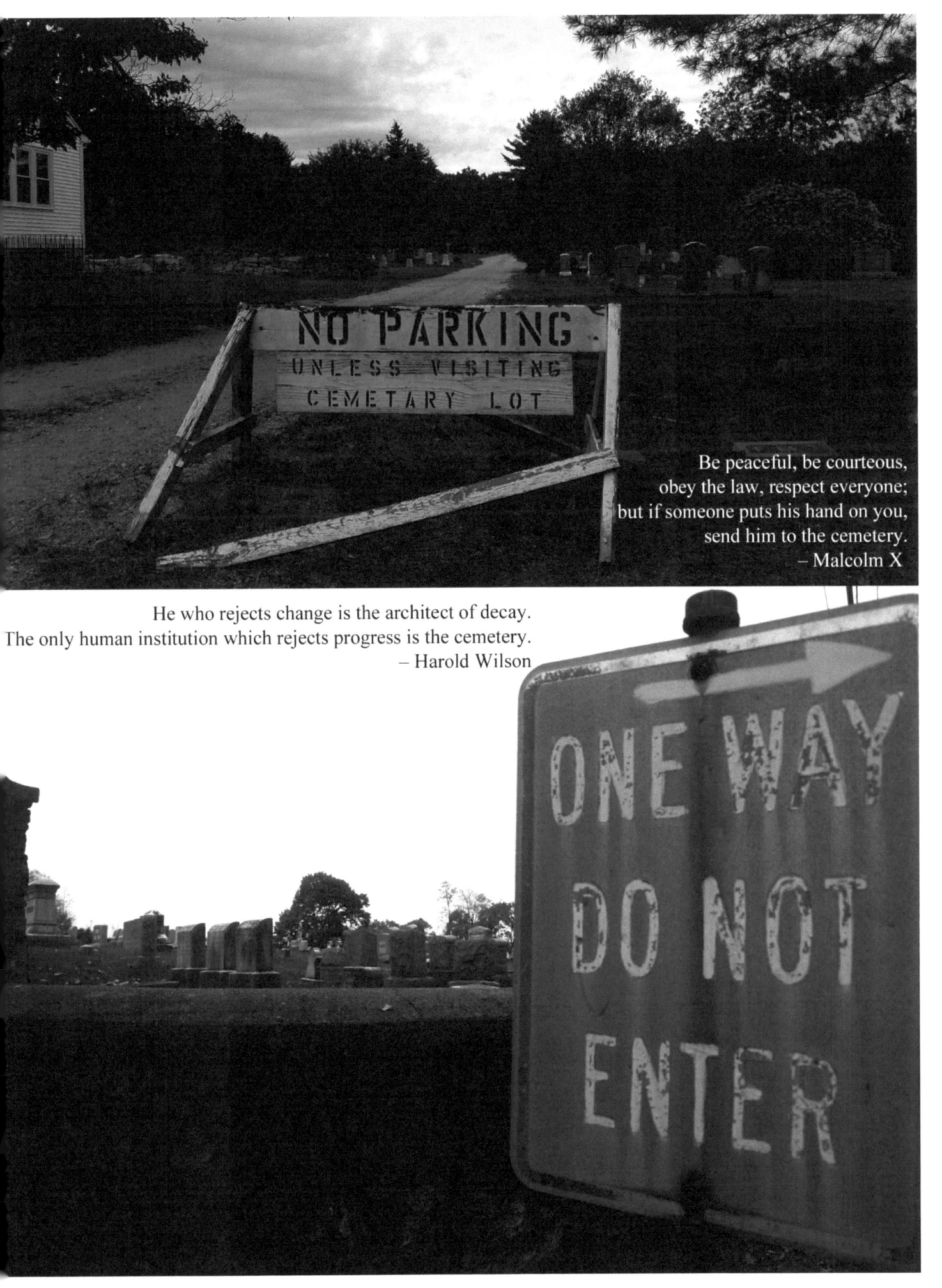

NO PARKING
UNLESS VISITING
CEMETARY LOT

Be peaceful, be courteous,
obey the law, respect everyone;
but if someone puts his hand on you,
send him to the cemetery.
– Malcolm X

He who rejects change is the architect of decay.
The only human institution which rejects progress is the cemetery.
– Harold Wilson

ONE WAY
DO NOT
ENTER

Every man should keep a fair-sized cemetery
in which to bury the faults of his friends
– Henry Ward Beecher

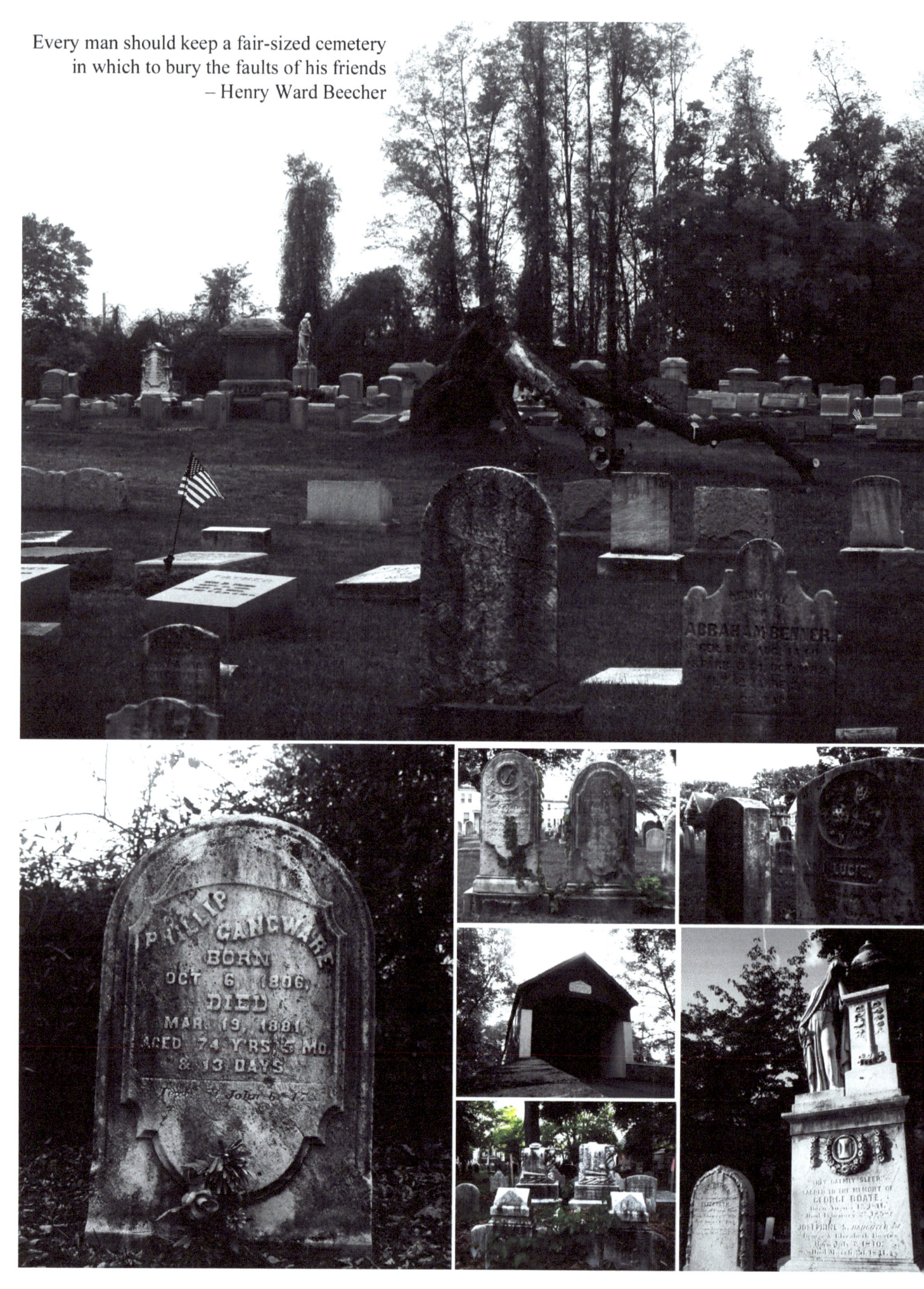

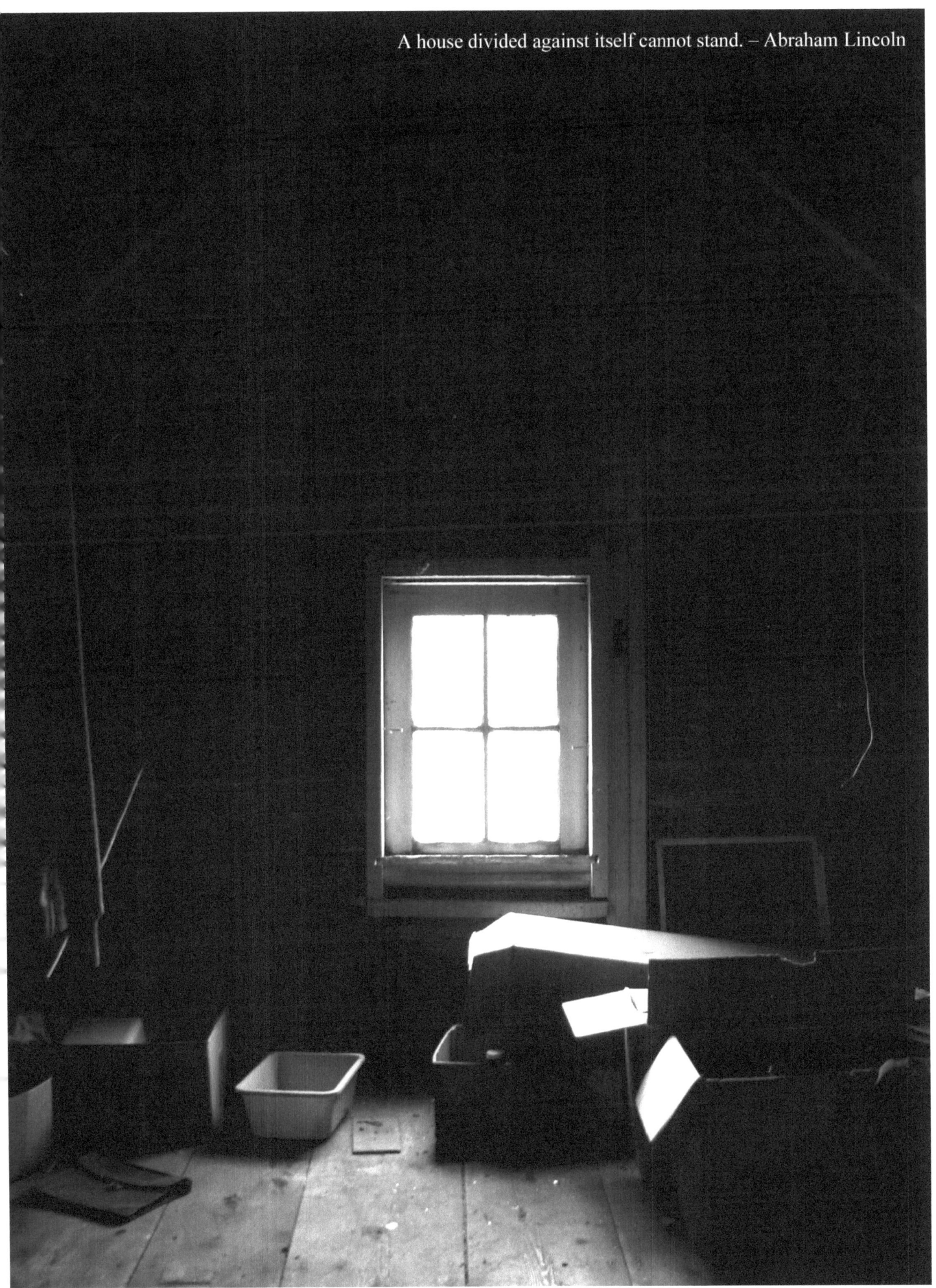

A house divided against itself cannot stand. – Abraham Lincoln

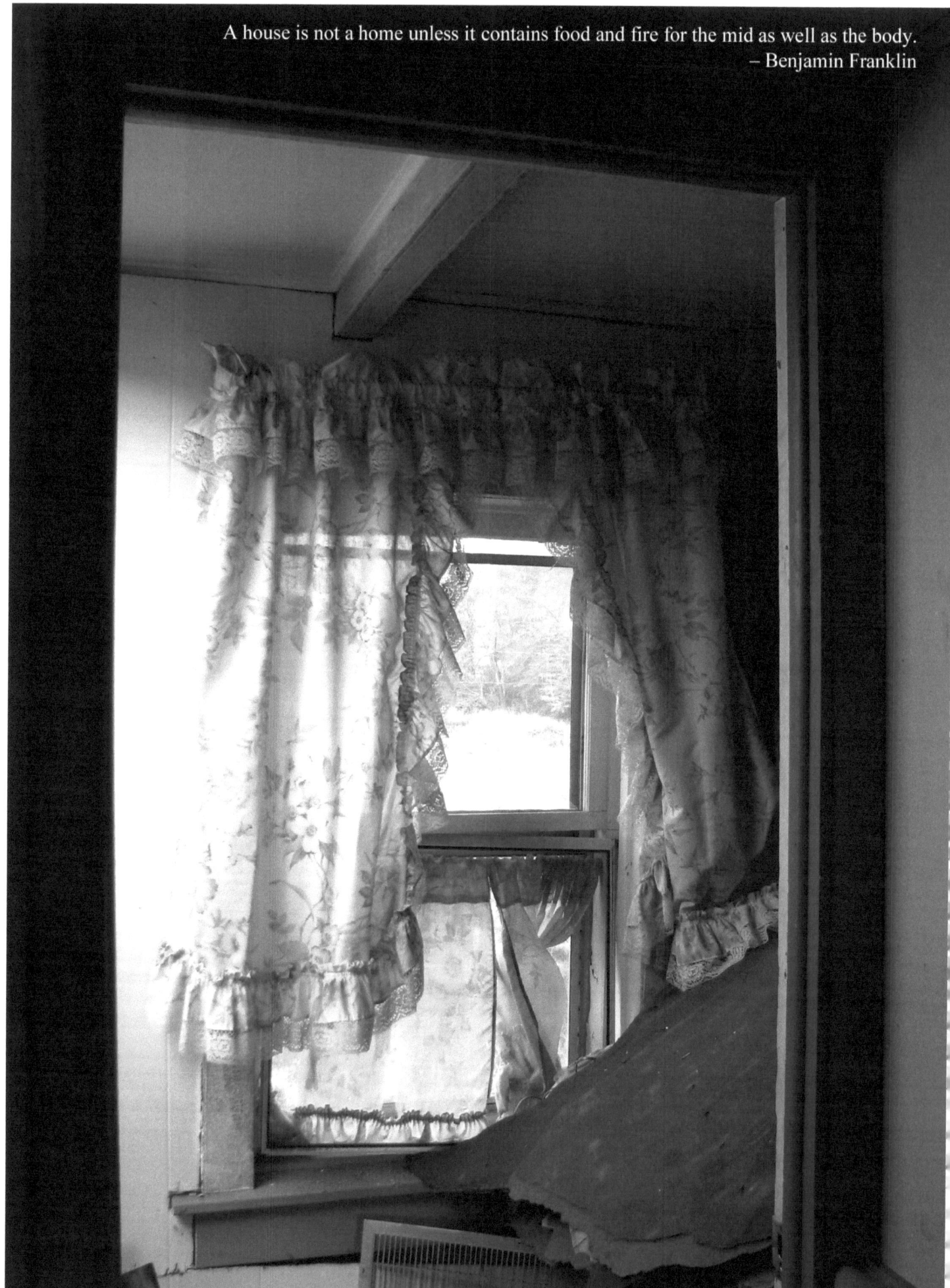

A house is not a home unless it contains food and fire for the mid as well as the body.
— Benjamin Franklin

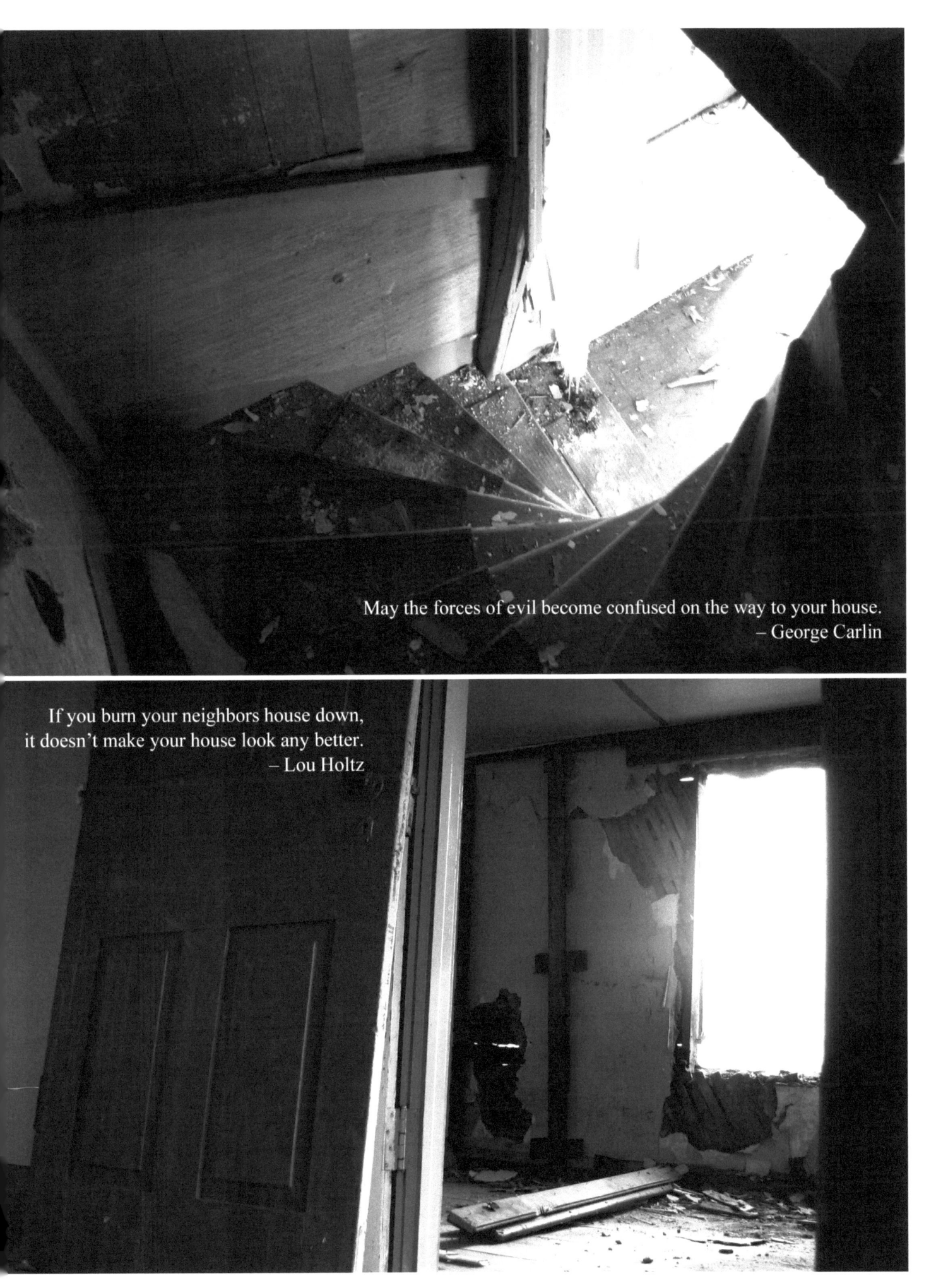

May the forces of evil become confused on the way to your house.
– George Carlin

If you burn your neighbors house down,
it doesn't make your house look any better.
– Lou Holtz

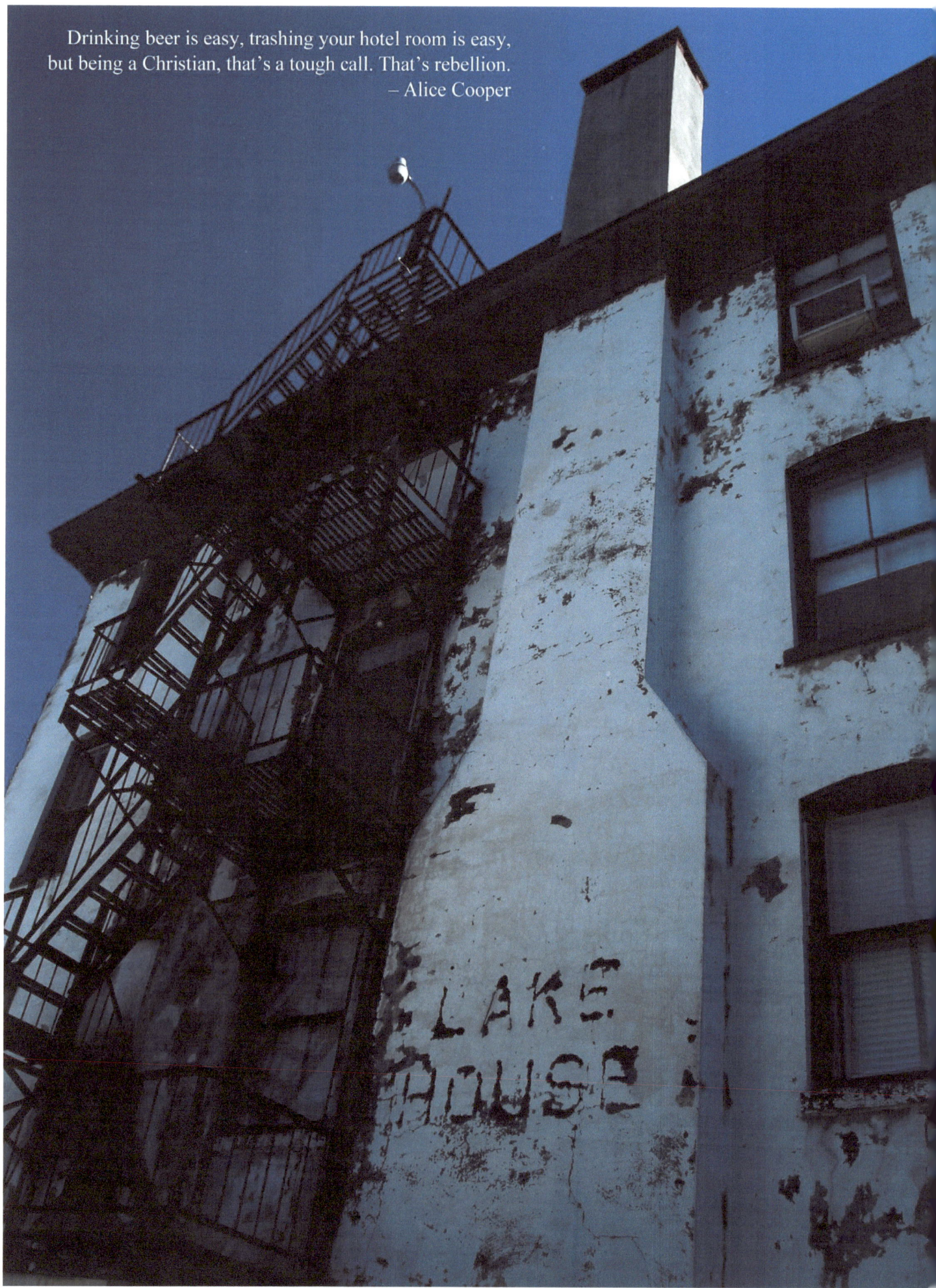

Drinking beer is easy, trashing your hotel room is easy,
but being a Christian, that's a tough call. That's rebellion.
— Alice Cooper

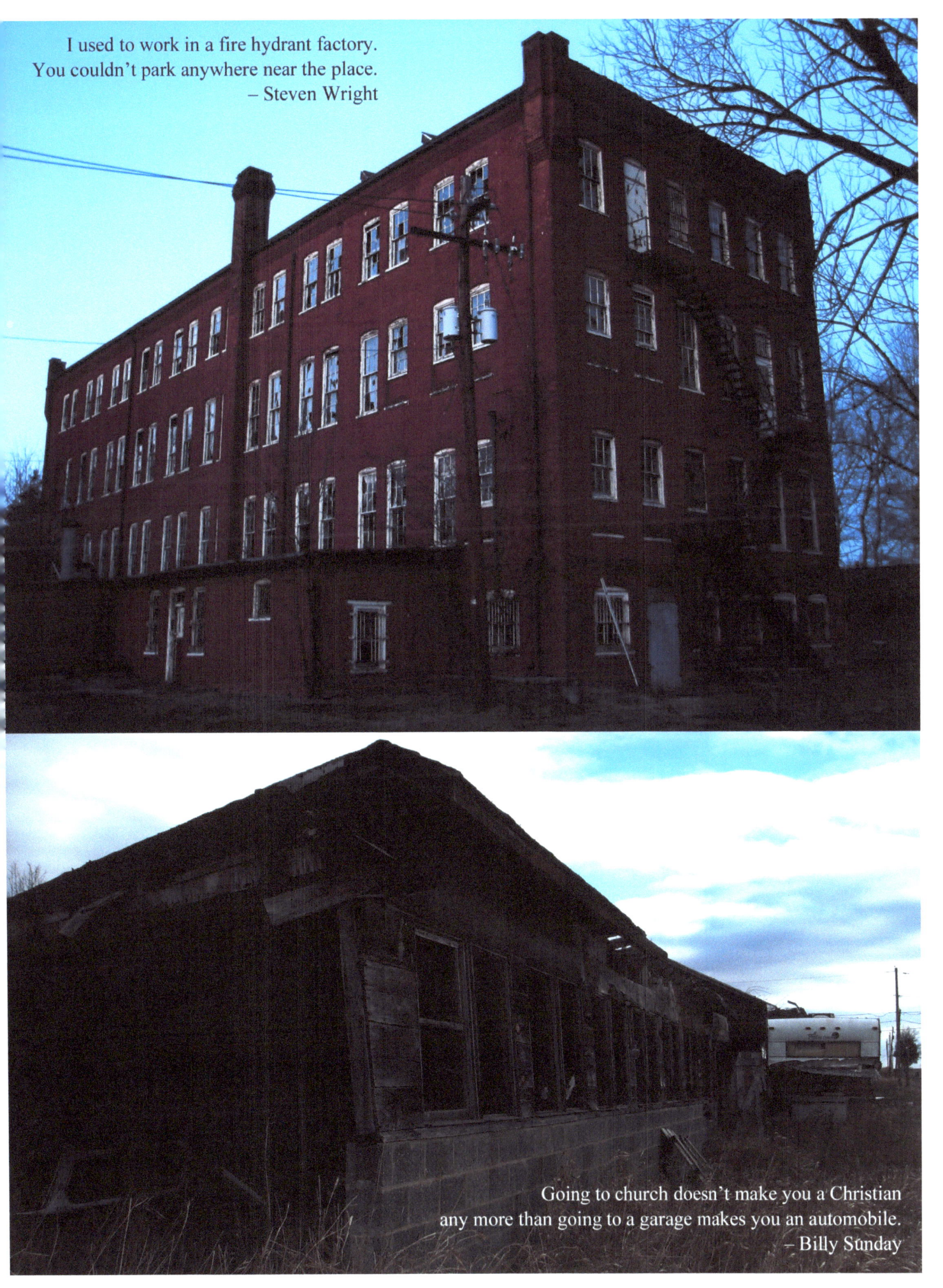

I used to work in a fire hydrant factory.
You couldn't park anywhere near the place.
— Steven Wright

Going to church doesn't make you a Christian
any more than going to a garage makes you an automobile.
— Billy Sunday

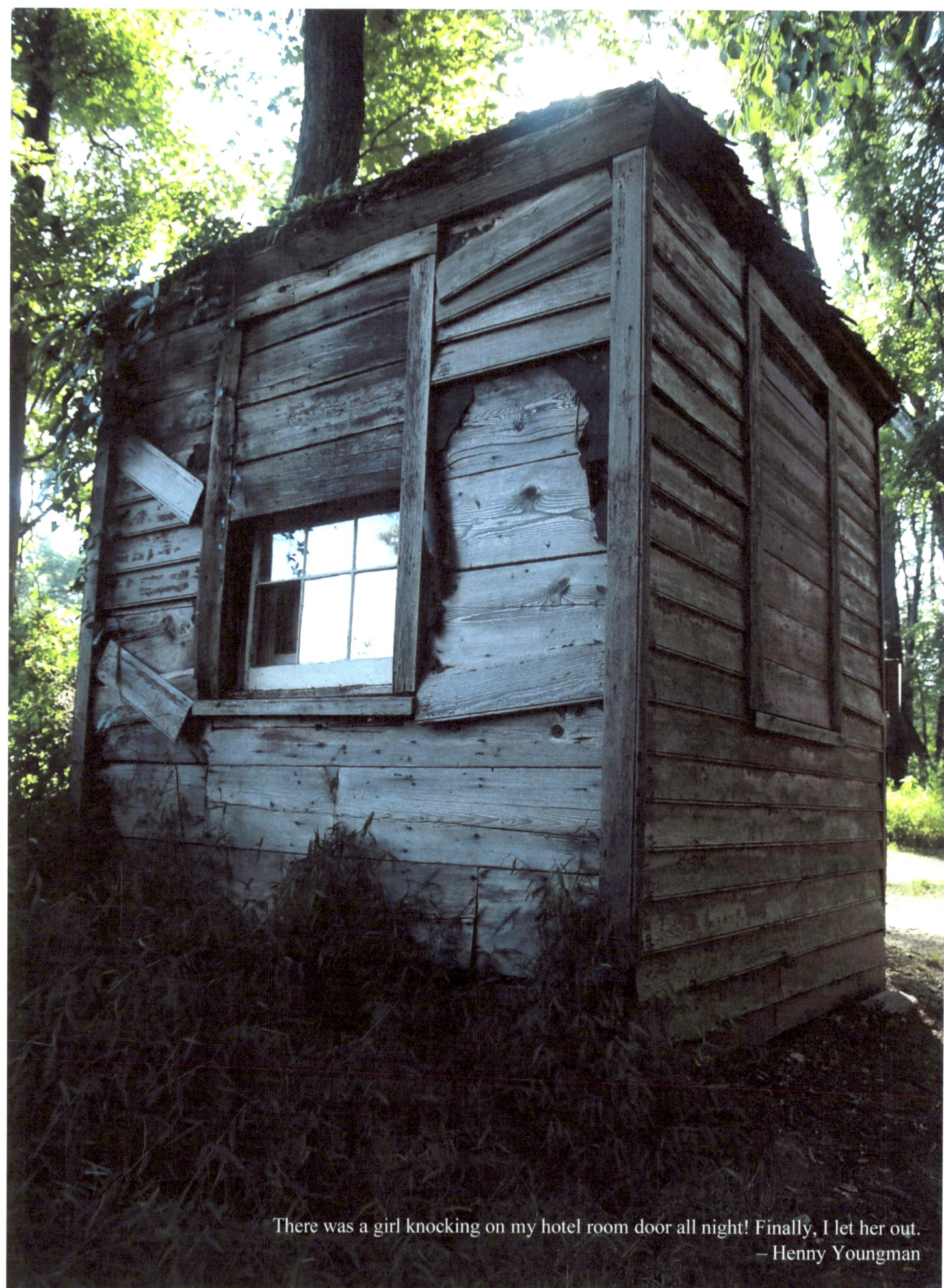

There was a girl knocking on my hotel room door all night! Finally, I let her out.
— Henny Youngman

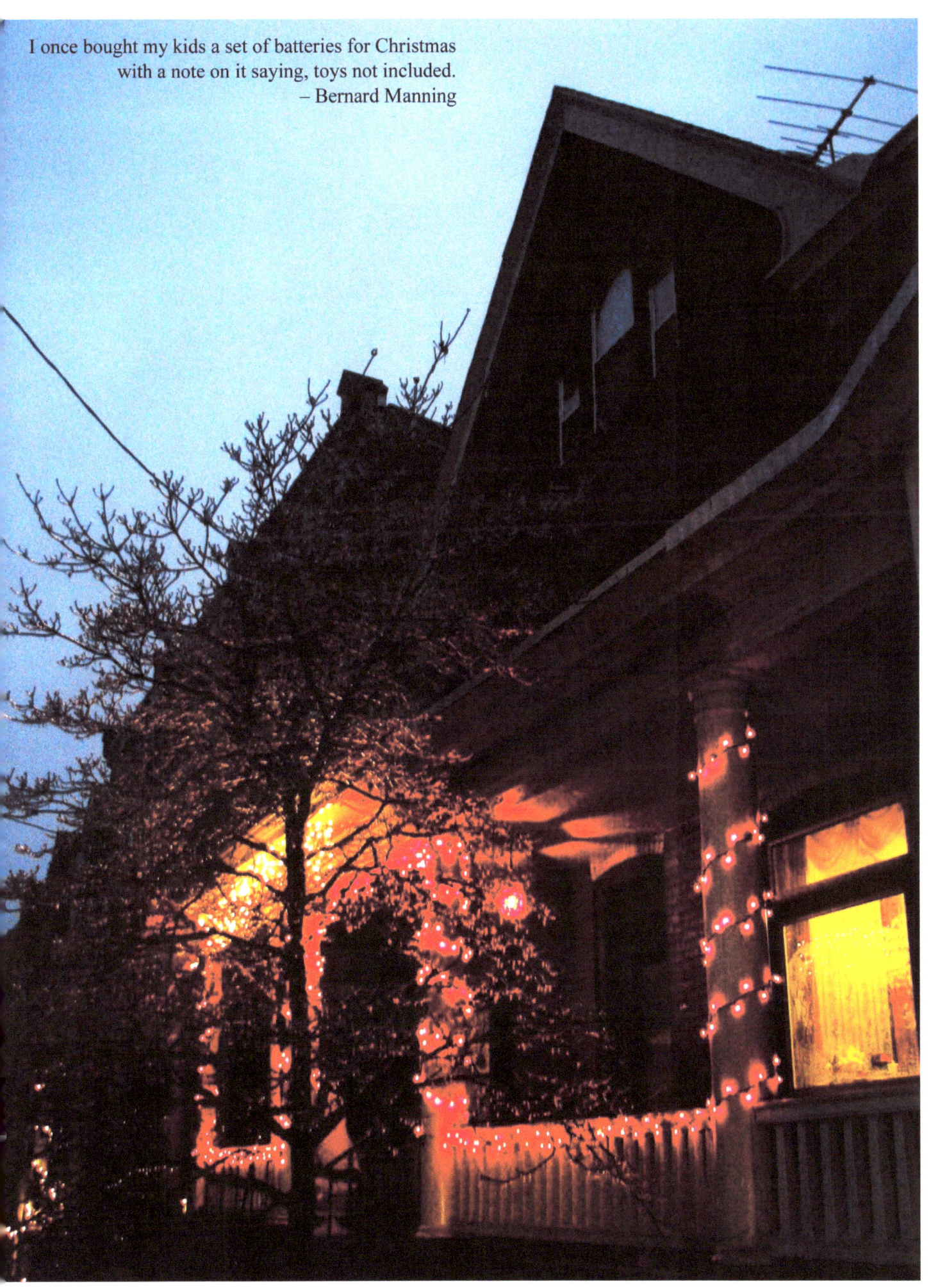

I once bought my kids a set of batteries for Christmas
with a note on it saying, toys not included.
– Bernard Manning

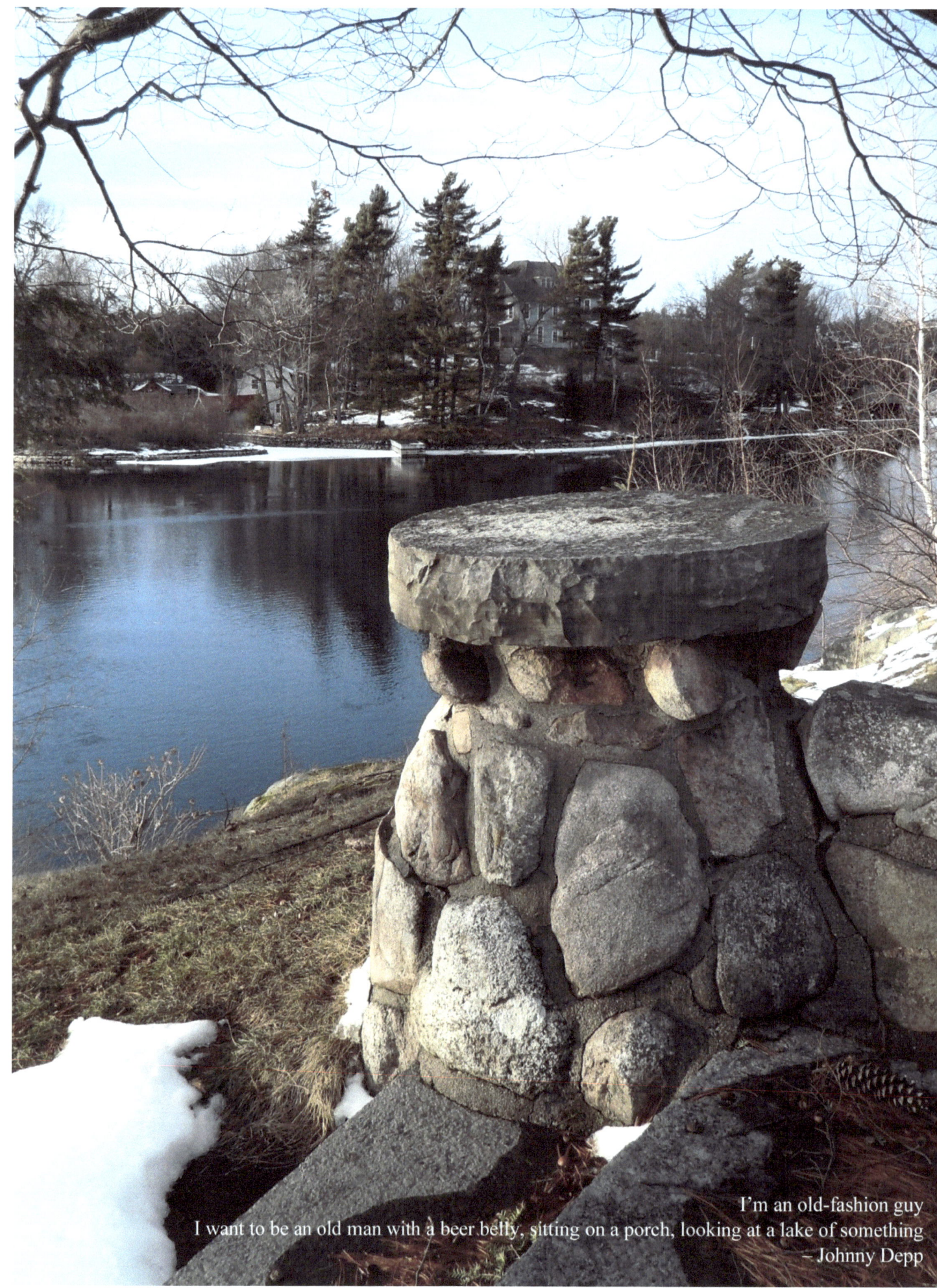

I'm an old-fashion guy
I want to be an old man with a beer belly, sitting on a porch, looking at a lake of something
– Johnny Depp

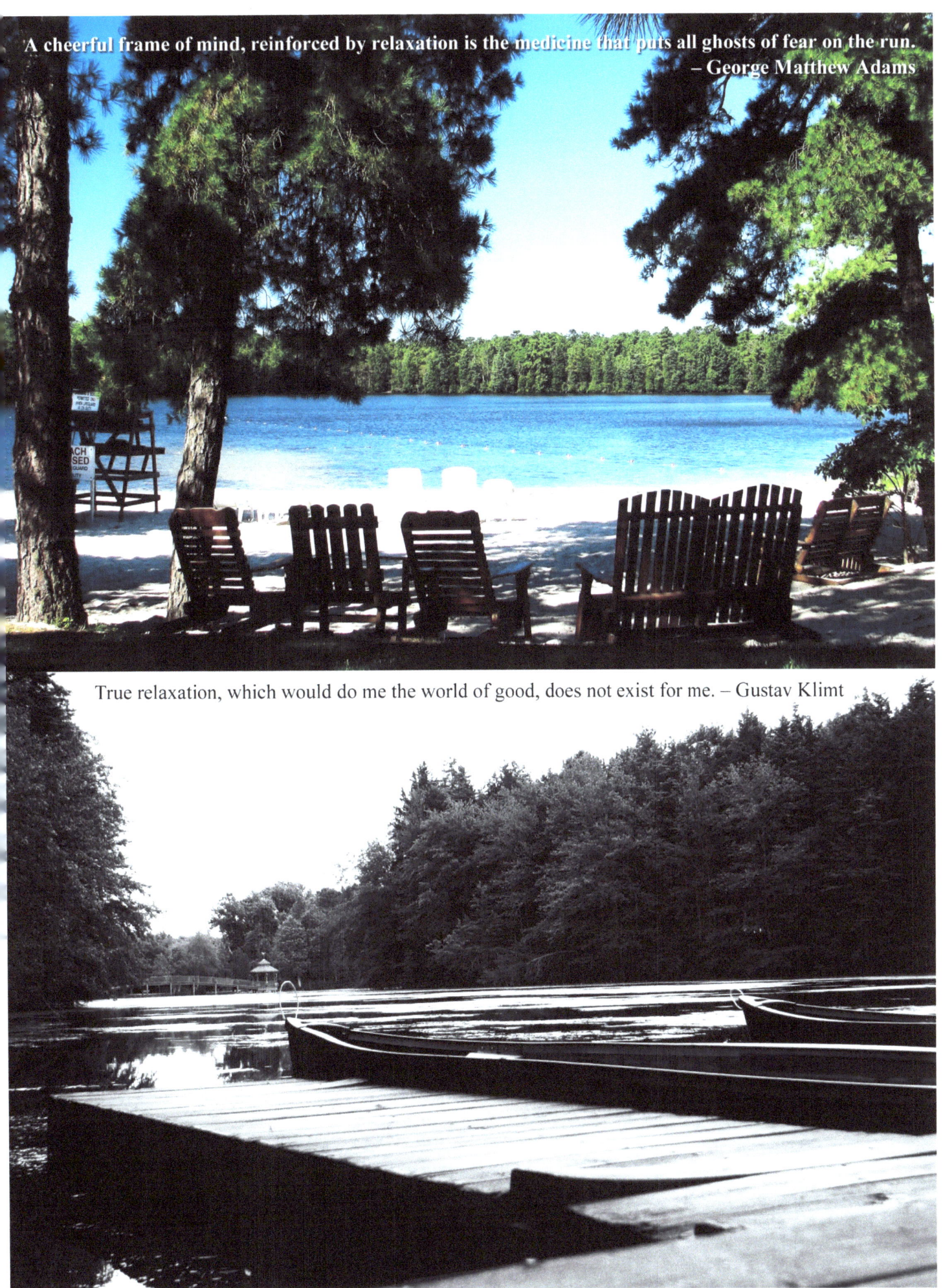

A cheerful frame of mind, reinforced by relaxation is the medicine that puts all ghosts of fear on the run.
– George Matthew Adams

True relaxation, which would do me the world of good, does not exist for me. – Gustav Klimt

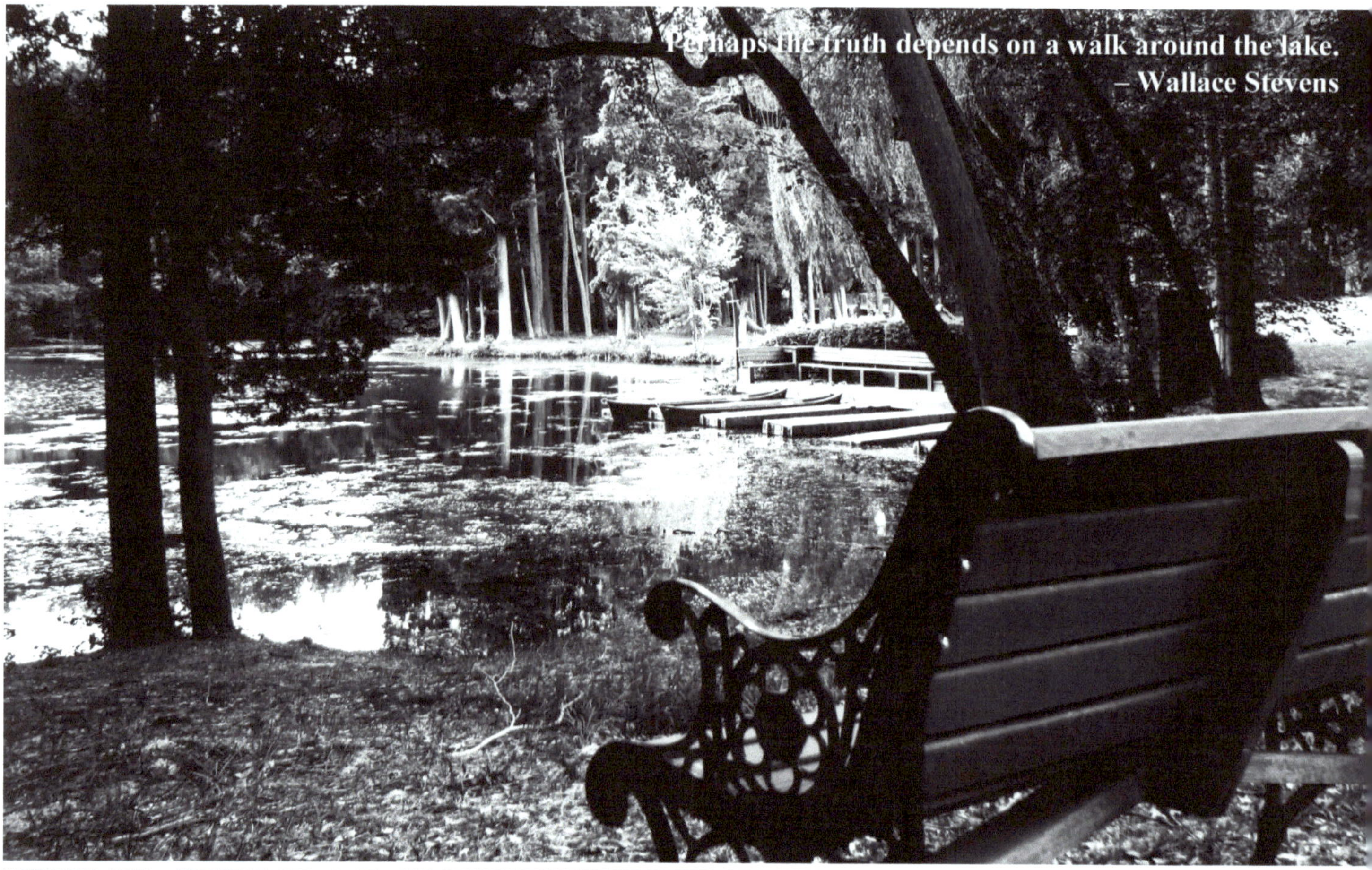

Perhaps the truth depends on a walk around the lake.
— Wallace Stevens

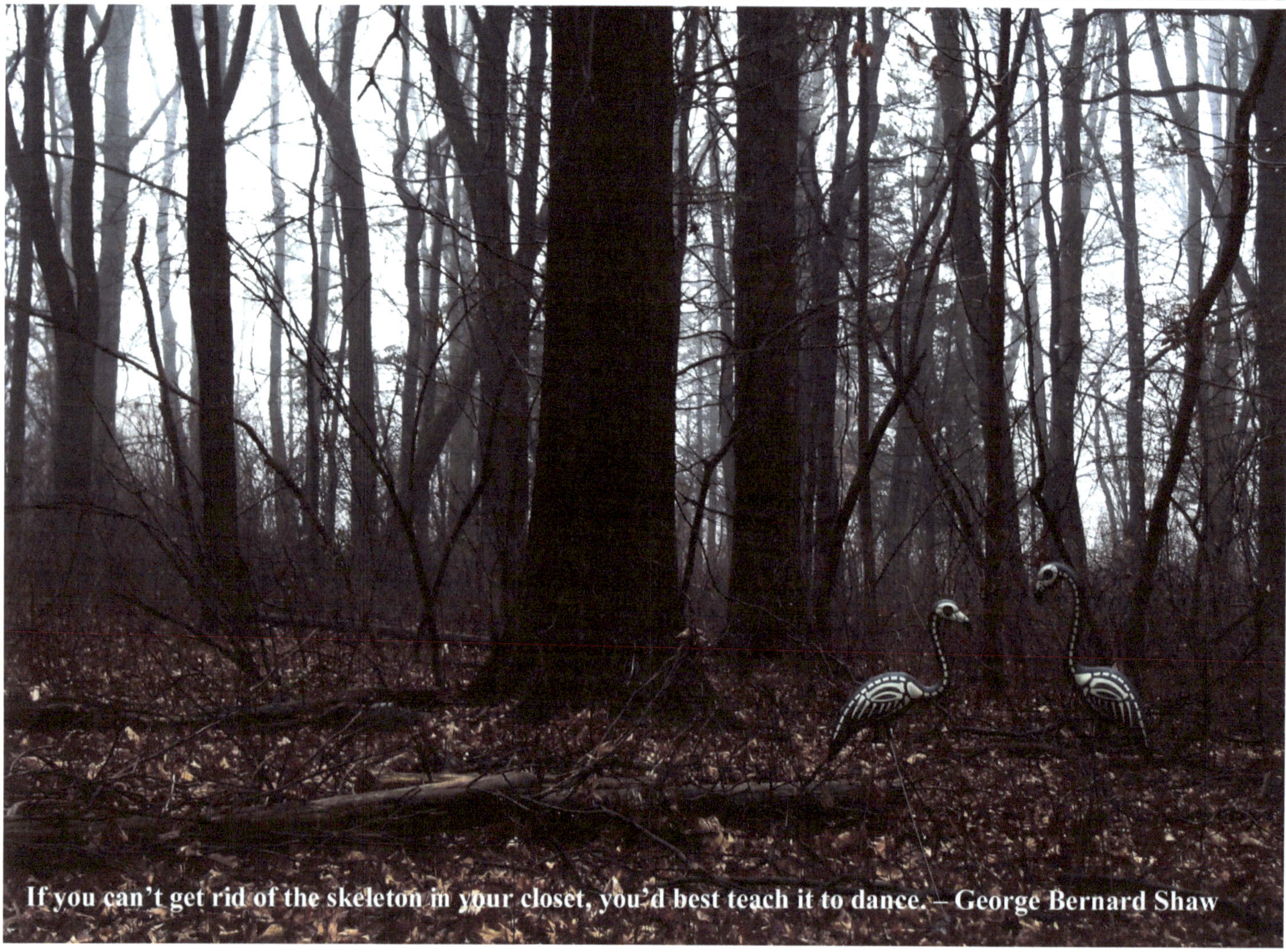

If you can't get rid of the skeleton in your closet, you'd best teach it to dance. — George Bernard Shaw

Every block of stone has a statue inside it and it is the task of the sculptor to discover it. - Michelangelo

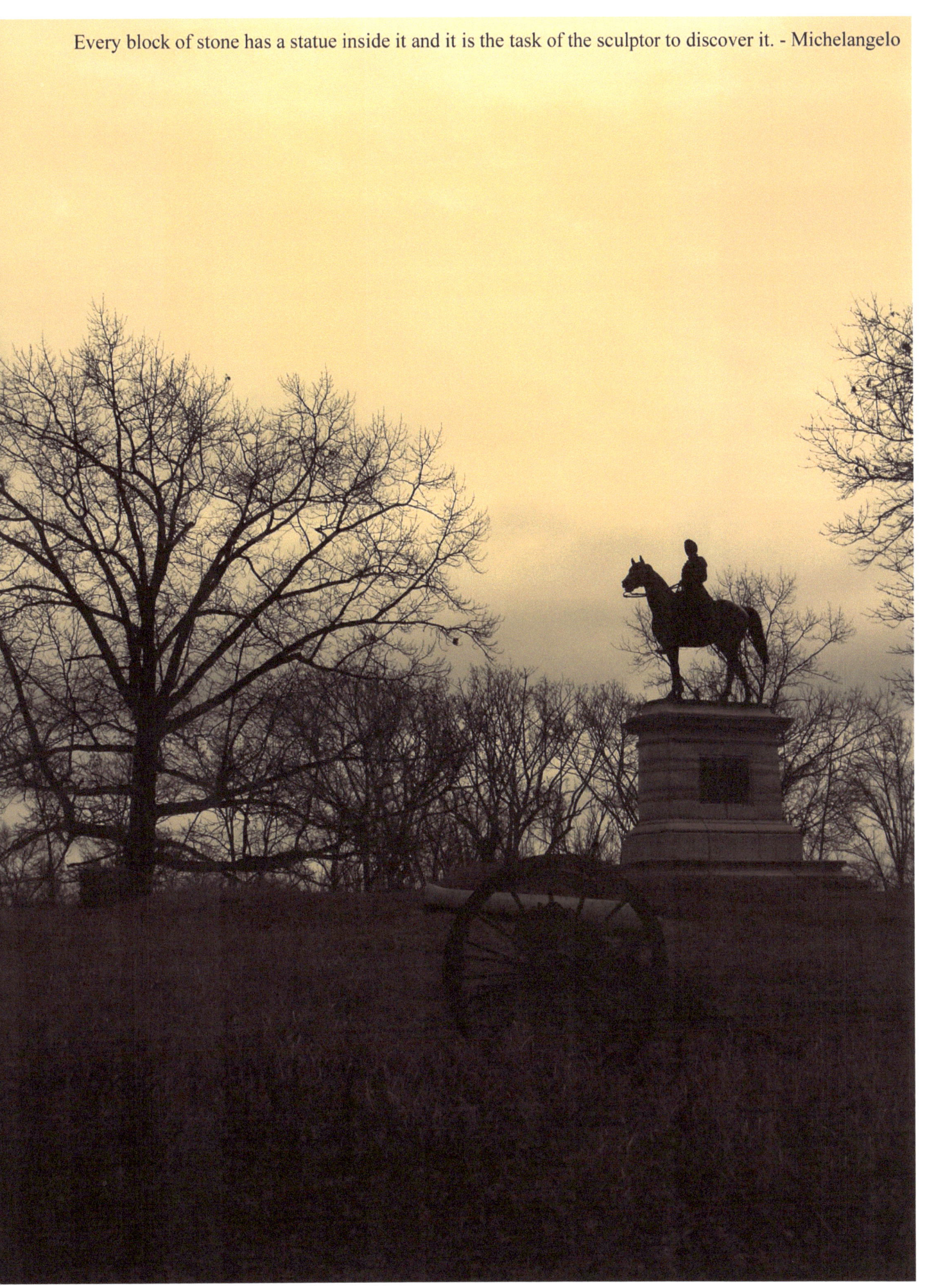

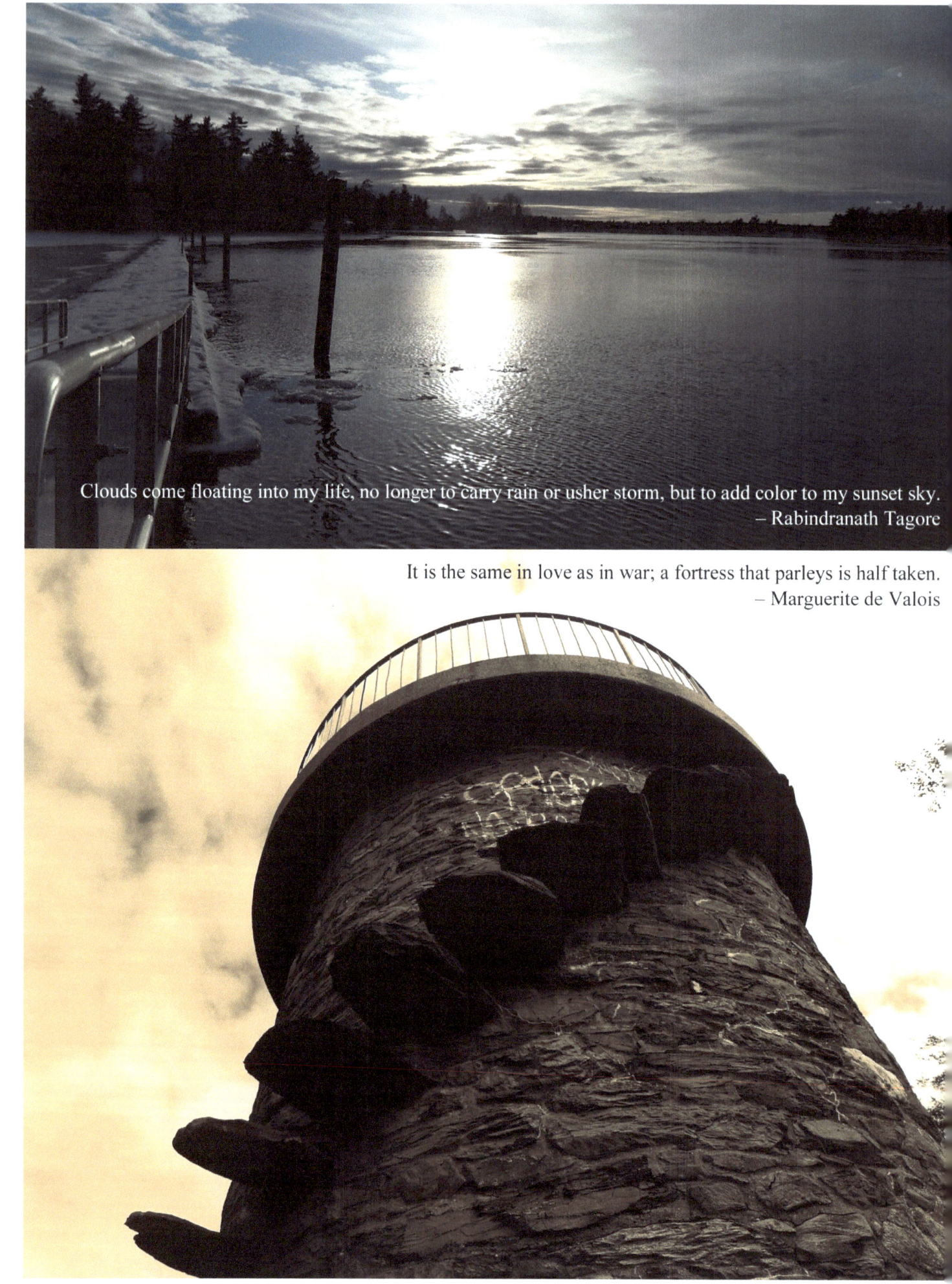

Clouds come floating into my life, no longer to carry rain or usher storm, but to add color to my sunset sky.
– Rabindranath Tagore

It is the same in love as in war; a fortress that parleys is half taken.
– Marguerite de Valois

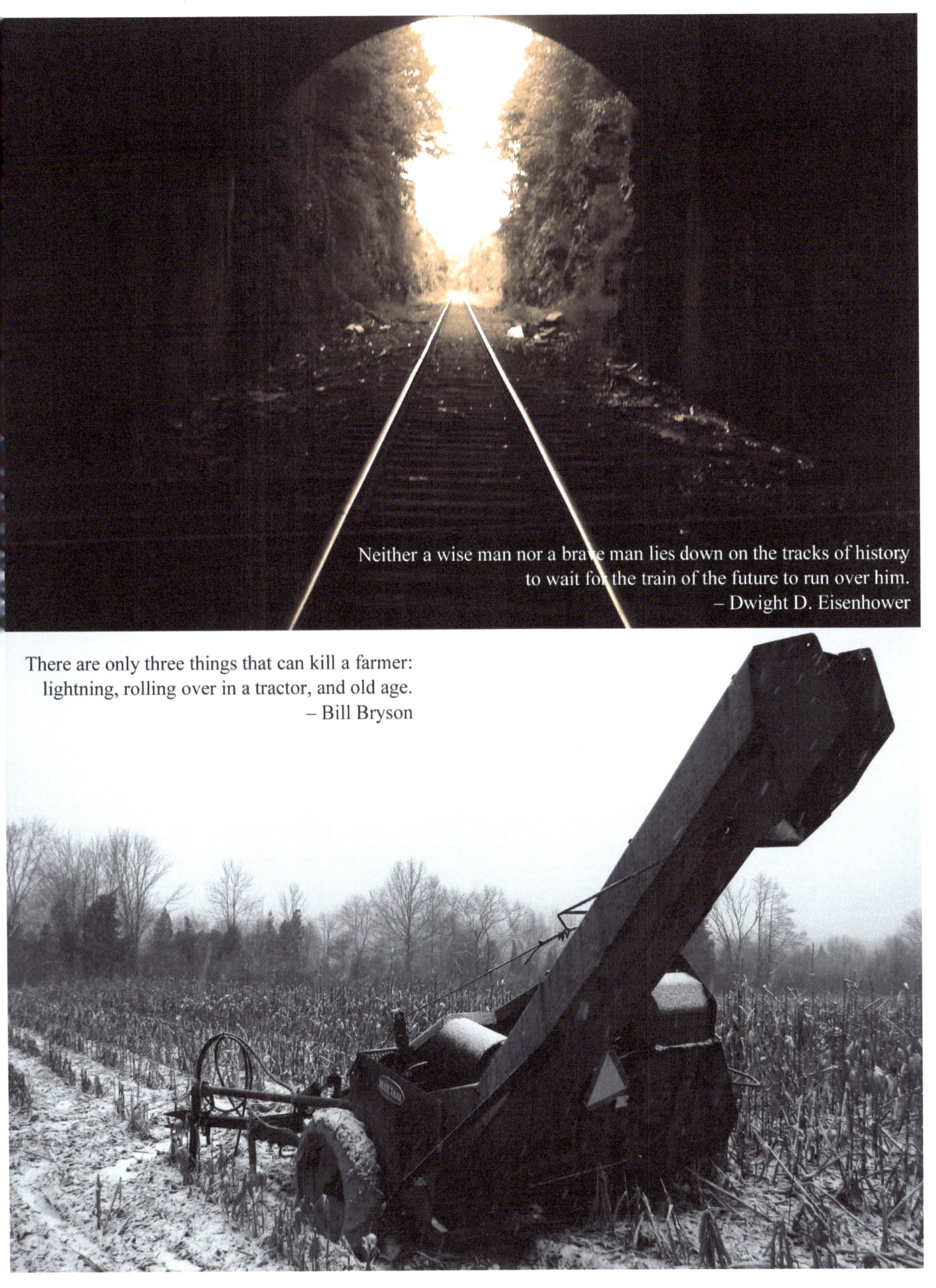

Neither a wise man nor a brave man lies down on the tracks of history
to wait for the train of the future to run over him.
– Dwight D. Eisenhower

There are only three things that can kill a farmer:
lightning, rolling over in a tractor, and old age.
– Bill Bryson

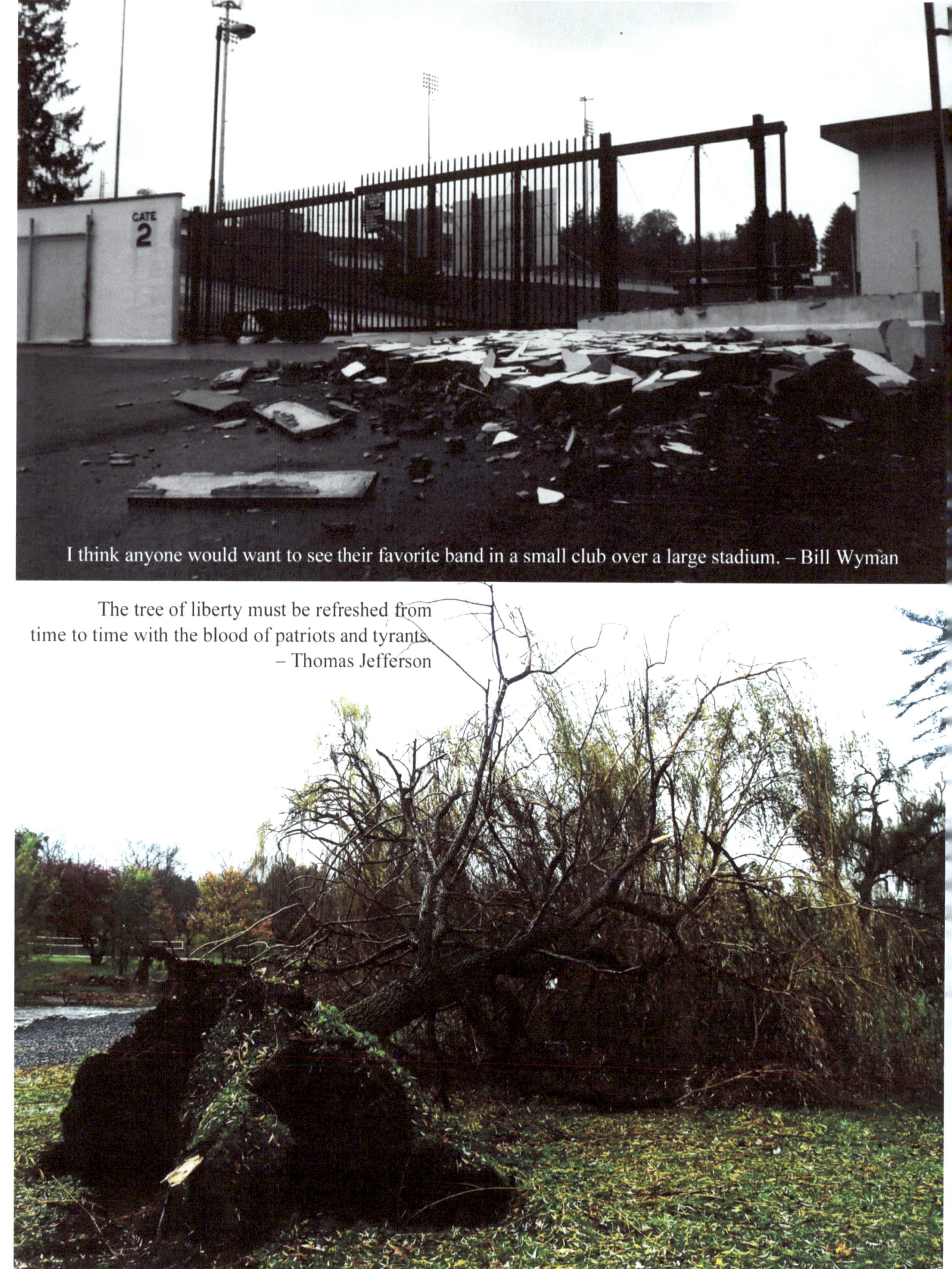

I think anyone would want to see their favorite band in a small club over a large stadium. – Bill Wyman

The tree of liberty must be refreshed from
time to time with the blood of patriots and tyrants.
– Thomas Jefferson

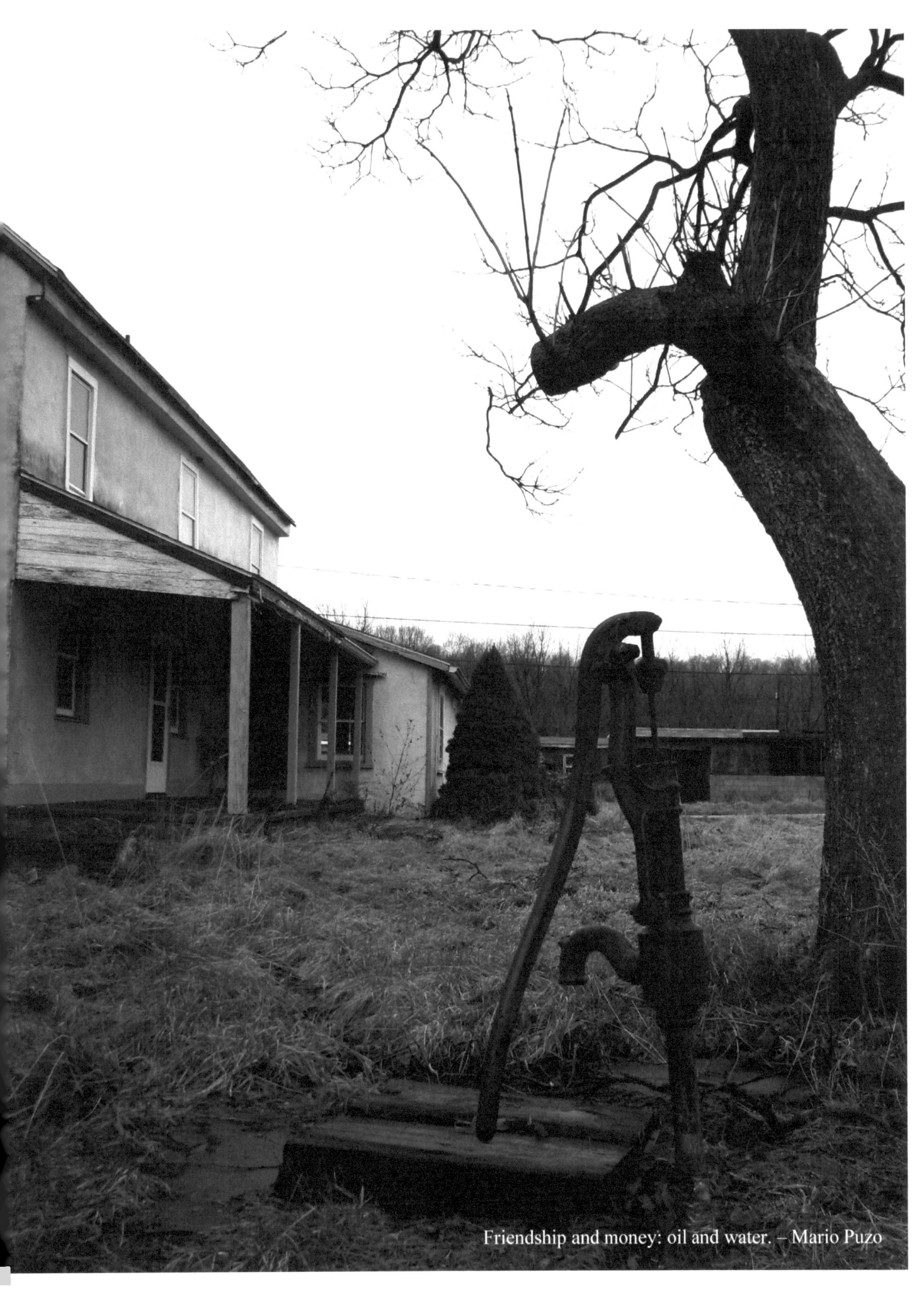

Friendship and money: oil and water. – Mario Puzo

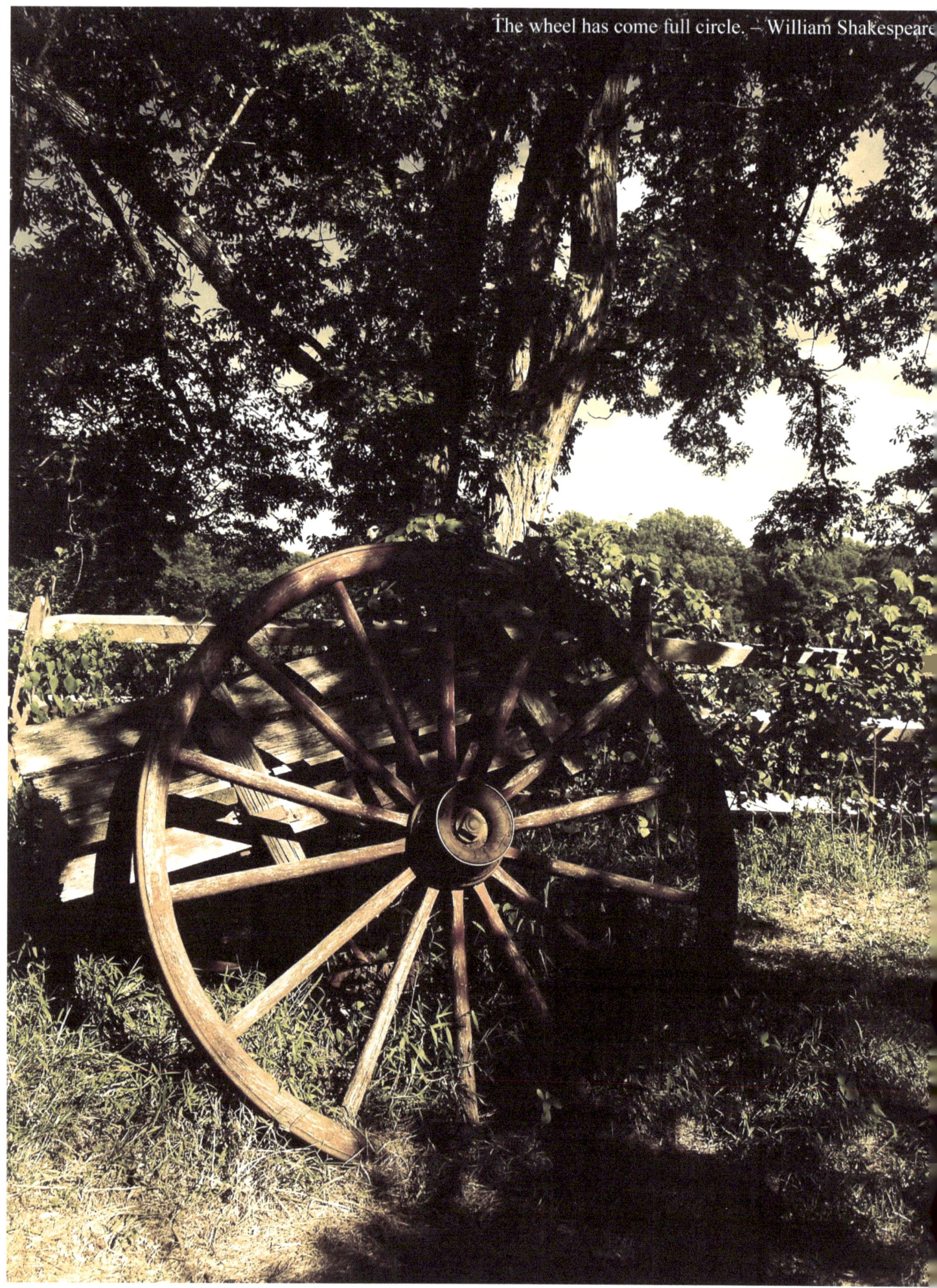

The wheel has come full circle. – William Shakespeare